To Dad from

W9-AQM-572

Christmas 2006

MARTYN LLOYD-JONES

Books by Martyn Lloyd-Jones:

Martyn Lloyd-Jones

A Family Portrait

CHRISTOPHER CATHERWOOD

Baker Books

A Division of Baker Book House Co
Grand Rapids, Michigan 49516

© 1994 by Christopher Catherwood

This edition published 1995 by Baker Books, a division of Baker Book House Company, P.O. Box 6287, Grand Rapids, MI 49516-6287, by special arrangement with Kingsway Publications, Lottbridge Drove, Eastbourne, East Sussex, England, BN23 6NT.

Printed in the United States of America

ISBN 0-8010-1042-X

To Paulette,
who is to me as Bethan Lloyd-Jones
was to her husband Martyn:
the perfect companion and the wisest counsellor.

Contents

Illustrations

LLOYD-JONES

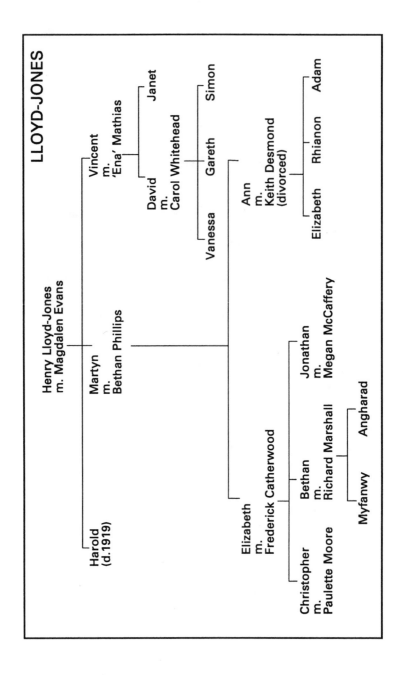

Henry Lloyd-Jones
m. Magdalen Evans

Harold
(d.1919)

Martyn
m.
Bethan Phillips

Vincent
m.
'Ena' Mathias

David
m.
Carol Whitehead

Janet

Vanessa

Gareth

Simon

Ann
m.
Keith Desmond
(divorced)

Elizabeth

Rhianon

Adam

Elizabeth
m.
Frederick Catherwood

Christopher
m.
Paulette Moore

Bethan
m.
Richard Marshall

Jonathan
m.
Megan McCaffery

Myfanwy

Angharad

PHILLIPS
(giving those mentioned in the text)

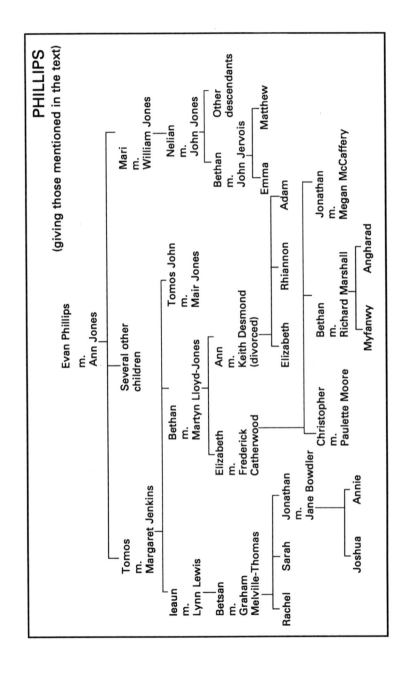

Acknowledgements

I would first of all like to thank my wife Paulette, who has been a wonderful help to me while writing this book. She has not only put up with holidays, weekends and evenings being devoted to this project, but has also been of considerable assistance in the writing process, reading every draft with great care and offering much wise advice. To her I give my deepest thanks for all her love and enthusiasm in completing this book.

Secondly, my family have also given me the greatest aid possible. In particular, my parents, Fred and Elizabeth Catherwood, have been invaluable, not just in terms of giving me their own memories of my grandfather—many such appear in this book—but also in terms of looking through all the drafts, offering advice and checking everything that I have said for accuracy. To them, therefore, my very special thanks for all that and for their support for the book and their warm, loving encouragement in the writing.

Other members of my family have also been of help, freely sharing their memories with me (I give their relationship to the Doctor in brackets). These are Bethan Marshall (eldest grand-daughter), Betsan Melville-Thomas (niece), Jonathan Melville-Thomas (great-nephew) and Bethan Jervois (cousin). I thank them all for their time and enthusiasm.

Lastly, I would like to thank my publisher, Richard Herkes, who has over the years become a close personal friend. He is the 'editor's editor' *par excellence*, the person without whom many a book would never have been written, but who has often not been given the credit he has deserved. He is a true mentor, someone who has taught me over many years all that a true editor should be. His enthusiasm for the Doctor's books over the past ten years has been of invaluable support and encouragement to the family, and in paying him due tribute here I do so not merely on account of this book, but also on behalf of the Doctor's family for all his commitment to the Doctor's literary ministry in recent times. The Christian world owes him a great debt, and I am delighted to use this opportunity to thank Richard for all he has done.

Introduction

When great men died in years gone by, there was a habit of commissioning two quite distinct biographies of their lives. One was the magisterial 'life and letters' that often ran into several volumes, and was sometimes written by a close colleague who had become as eminent as the subject himself. It listed in considerable detail all that the Great Man had done, his public life, and the way in which he had transformed the world. But then there was the other kind, written at a more personal level, that described the man himself, rather than what that man had done. Such a biography is by no means exhaustive, but it does give one an inside view of the human being behind the Great Man.

When it comes to Martyn Lloyd-Jones, nothing could possibly replace the magisterial two-volume biography by Iain Murray, written with the Doctor's consent and much of it researched in the Doctor's lifetime. This volume here would not pretend to do that. Rather it aims to do something completely different.

This book is designed to complete the picture; to portray the private man behind the Great Man. What was Doctor Martyn Lloyd-Jones *really* like? What kind of person was he with friends and above all with his family? Many have a rather austere picture of him—the man in the black Geneva gown who never cracked jokes in the pulpit. Yet with friends and family he was one of the most enjoyable people you could possibly wish for—and his jokes were legendary.

To those around him, he was the kindest of men, someone who radiated enormous warmth, and who was immensely loyal to his own. Furthermore, as we shall see, he always believed in taking people as they were, rather than as others would like them to be. He never made conformity with his views a test of affection, since to his family he gave his love unreservedly. Unless one understands this of him, one does not get a true picture of the extraordinary man of God who was Martyn Lloyd-Jones.

As we will see, there are many too who would like to claim Dr Lloyd-Jones—'the Doctor' to most who knew him—for themselves. This is of course true of all great men, and he was no exception. Often the opinions that he was supposed to hold were mutually contradictory! Iain Murray's life of the Doctor also has its views, and what makes it command respect is that its author is quite open about where he and the Doctor disagreed. Unlike some, Murray does not attempt to suppress any of the Doctor's opinions, whether he agrees with them personally or not.

This biography does the same thing, from a different angle. It looks at the Doctor and what he taught from the perspective of those closest to him—his own family. With us, he could be completely frank about what he thought—and we could be equally frank with him. Not only did he not mind this, he positively encouraged it. In writing this book, I made sure to ask other members of the family what they thought, so what you have here is a considered view representing the opinions of more than one person. (Not all members of the family wanted to be included in this book, and I have respected this by leaving them out. Those who did want to be included, and whose memories can be placed 'on the record', are thanked in the acknowledgements.)

This book does not, therefore, profess to be definitive. For that the two-volume official life is irreplaceable, and people wanting such detail can always turn to it. Inevitably, therefore, this has meant that several of the things the Doctor was involved with have been dealt with briefly—such as the Puritan Conference and the founding of the Banner of Truth. Other areas of his life, such as the Evangelical Movement of Wales and the Evangelical Library are only mentioned in passing, if at all.

Rather, I have concentrated on either those aspects of his life which impinged on the family—such as Westminster Chapel or the IFES (in which several of us were involved)—or on those things that show the kind of man he was. This means that some parts of his public life are left out, but considerable prominence is given to the kind of grandfather he was. Rather than portraying each individual tree, I have tried to give an aerial view of the forest, and have concentrated on those trees that were in the shade for the official biography. So if, for example, someone who loved hearing the Doctor at the Bala conferences picks up this book and finds nothing about them, that is why.

But my hope is that having read this biography, you will have a much better sense of the man: who he was, what made him what he was and what he was like in private, away from the public gaze. He was a remarkable man by all accounts, a larger-than-life figure of the kind by which we are seldom blessed. To have known him as we did within his family was the rarest of privileges, and we shall not see his like again. If you get only a small sense of the bigness of the man—of the breadth of his vision, of his compassion, his wisdom, his sheer warmth and depth of affection, and above all his ability to give one a sense of the glory of God and the greatness of our salvation in Christ—then my writing this book and your reading it will not have been in vain.

I
The Early Years
1899–1927

David Martyn Lloyd-Jones was born in Cardiff on the
20th December 1899, the middle son of a poor but highly
able dairy shop owner, Henry Lloyd-Jones, and his wife
Magdalen, the daughter of a farming family. His father
had been born a simple Jones, but on marriage had
combined his last Christian name with his surname—
keeping apart from the Joneses, you might say. His wife
was born with another Welsh surname, Evans, so their
son's ancestry was entirely Celtic. Being born at the end
of the 1800s always made his age easy to remember: he
was, except for eleven days, always the same age as the
year.

As a child, the middle Lloyd-Jones son preferred to be
known as David, his first name, becoming known as
Martyn only later in life. He was thus always D. Martyn
Lloyd-Jones, the 'D' being his name rather than an abbre-
viation for the doctorate he was later to earn. (For sake of
simplicity, though, we will refer to him as Martyn.)

Family background

Martyn had two brothers. The older, Harold, was very
clever, and was thinking of becoming a solicitor. The
younger one, Vincent, went on to become a distinguished
High Court judge. There is a wonderful picture of the

three small Lloyd-Jones boys. Harold, the eldest, is in a smart little suit. He is looking very handsome and dignified, as all big brothers should. Vincent is still in baby clothes, but is evidently feeling a little uneasy. This is because the cheery, slightly chubby middle brother, Martyn, has been regularly pinching him and generally creating the kind of disturbance that made taking the picture almost impossible!

All three boys were academically bright. This was nurtured by the considerable encouragement they received from their father Henry. In another age he would have been a professor. But he never had the chance that his sons were to enjoy, nor the money that was then required, so he ended up as the manager of a village general store. The intellectual, reflective side of Martyn Lloyd-Jones, as well as his passion for books, was from his father. The drive and fighting temperament he inherited from his mother's family, the Evanses. His grandfather, David Evans, ran a farm at Llwyncadfor in Cardiganshire. As well as the farm, they had a singularly successful stud, whose horses regularly won awards. Old Evans was much feared and was not crossed easily. It was this unique mix that was to create the character of the preacher and Christian leader that was later to be: passionate intellect, zealous introvert, bookish inspirer of thousands.

Much of this was encouraged by the family atmosphere at home, which was one of lively debate. Politics was a major preoccupation in the Lloyd-Jones household. All of them were Liberals, but their discussions reflected the divisions within that great Party that were later to split it and exile it from Government for good. Henry supported the more moderate H. H. Asquith, an Englishman, and, like many others of that persuasion, he embraced the 'new theology' which closely mixed social action with non-conformist churchmanship. By contrast young

Martyn preferred to support the fiery radical on the left of the party, the Welsh orator David Lloyd-George.

When he was five the family moved to Llangeitho, a small town in Cardiganshire (now Dyfed), in the heart of Welsh South Wales. Apart from being picturesque, it was also steeped in history, and of a very influential kind. Llangeitho was where the great eighteenth-century preacher Daniel Rowlands had been based for many years. Many of his views were later to be held by its new young inhabitant, and if there is such a thing as a spirit of a place, in this case it was wholly benign. As an adult Martyn was often to go back there, not just because of its happy associations, but because of the profound sense of history and of continuity with the great Christian saints of the past that such places gave him.

When I was a small child he took me there. There is a photo of me, trying in vain to imitate the outstretched arm of the statue of Daniel Rowlands just behind us, with my grandfather, slightly camera shy, drinking in his heritage.

Early childhood

Martyn's early childhood in Wales was a happy one. Initially he preferred sport to schoolwork, and played many a game of football with the other boys. Although he was never particularly gifted in this area, he continued to enjoy watching sport to the end of his life. Sometimes this combined a love of outdoor activity with his Welsh heritage, such as sheep dog trials, where the shepherd gets the dogs to steer the sheep into the pen. But often it was something more prosaic, like snooker. This interest in sport surprised many of his friends and admirers, but I think that what caused it was a love of skill. He liked sports where the player had to think, to reflect on tactics, to weigh up the possibilities.

Some adventures

Llangeitho, like many small Welsh communities, was a friendly environment. As the Lloyd-Jones home was also a store, it was a particularly social place. All kinds of folk would come in, perfect training for the different species of humanity who would one day see him as a pastor. He used to maintain that the villages of South Wales produced more than the usual share of 'characters' than the rather anonymous suburbs and cities of the late twentieth century. To be described by him as a 'character' was always a huge compliment. He liked his friends larger than life, and he was of course just that himself. Family birthdays, when he was older, were times of reminiscence, and he and his brother Vincent would enjoy regaling the younger generation of tales of their youth in Wales, of what was, by then, a different era, so fast had technology changed the world in which he lived.

One such story featured the village blacksmith who, it was said, held the record for long distance spitting! Martyn was also an excellent horse rider and he particularly enjoyed going up to his grandfather Evans' farm and riding the ponies. There is a wonderful early photo of him on one, grinning impishly from ear to ear, and looking not unlike his youngest grandson Adam at the same age. Grandfather Evans could get rather irascible, and Martyn was one of the very few who used to dare enter the room while he was still asleep.

In 1908 he had a special treat. Most transport in those days was still by horse, or by train from the larger towns. But one day young Martyn was able to ride in one of the earliest ever makes of car. A trip to London and back in those days was an epic journey enough in itself—but by car! On the way back, the car had a puncture, so the party stopped at a little bicycle shop in Oxford. Its owner was a Mr Morris—later world famous as Lord Nuffield, the founder of Morris cars, including the Mini.

But Martyn's halcyon early days came to an end in 1909. In fact they very nearly ended altogether. There was a fire in the family store, and nine-year-old Martyn survived only by being thrown from an upstairs window into a blanket below. His grandfather hinted to him that times were going to be much harder for the family, and little Martyn fully understood the consequences. He was now a very serious and studious young boy.

Away to school

In 1911 he won the second scholarship to the county intermediate school in the nearby town of Tregaron. Because of the distance he was no longer able to live at home, so he was obliged to join his older brother Harold in his lodgings in the town from Monday to Friday. He became desperately homesick, and always regarded his time in Tregaron as basically unhappy.

This also gave him a lifelong antagonism to the strange English upper-class habit of sending their children, often at a tender age, away to boarding school. When he was a leader of British evangelicalism, many of England's fore-most Evangelicals were still the products of what the English quaintly call the 'public school system'. The Doctor felt that it bred a very superficial type, often unable to cope with normal emotions, as the ethos of the 'stiff upper lip' demanded that all such emotion be crushed. This was in sharp distinction to the Welsh attitude, where tough men could and often did cry with-out regarding it as betraying their masculinity.

This gave the Doctor a natural affinity with those from the USA and Third World countries, whose healthy attitude to emotions matched his own. It also meant that, unlike some English Anglicans, he was not to be automatically threatened by the emotion displayed in the charismatic renewal movement. On the other hand, his was a balanced view and he never allowed his emotions, with which he had always been in touch, completely to overcome his head, as happened with some.

Boarding school, he felt, also broke up the family, and children were away from their parents at their most formative age. The Doctor was always a family man—his immediate and wider family meant a lot to him, and were a constant priority in his life. Even when he was a world-famous preacher, his grandchildren still had a very important claim on his time. However trivial their needs were to the average adult, they mattered to them so they mattered equally to him. He always took children at their own valuation, which meant that he got on very well with them—not just because he was at ease with children, but because he was never condescending. The very idea that the Lord would give you children only for you to send them away at a tender age was incomprehensible to him.

His dislike of boarding schools had another consequence too. Both his nephew David Lloyd-Jones and myself were to go on to attend Westminster School, the illustrious school in London that is part of Westminster Abbey. But we were day boys—the Doctor was not going to have us go through the same agonies at boarding school as he had suffered as a child. My father had never particularly enjoyed being a boarder at Shrewsbury, the boys' school near the Welsh borders. But like many public schoolboys before him, he had always been told it was necessary to make him into a real man. He was never convinced, though, and soon found an ally in his father-in-law, because all this was stuff and nonsense—a view for which I have been very grateful ever since!

At school itself, despite all his homesickness, young Martyn thrived academically. It dawned on him slowly that he was not just clever, but very clever indeed.

A love of history

Although he was eventually to specialise in the scientific disciplines, his favourite teacher was S. M. Powell, the history master. One of the problems that twentieth-century Evangelicals have is their woeful lack of knowledge of history. Did anything happen before 1900? Before 1950 even? Yet, whether we realise it or not, where we are now is a result of a long and often complex historical process. And we often make mistakes because we fail to see where exactly the same mistakes have been made before. But Martyn's love of church history remained all his life, and passionately so. For him, one could not understand the present without knowing the past. History was the wonderful story of the providence of God working among his people, blessing them, warning them. Through all his long ministry the Doctor urged his listeners to read history, to see how God intervened in great and amazing ways.

Not only that, but the lives of individual Christians could teach us so much. They wrestled with the same problems as we did. Maybe circumstances were different, but humans do not change from one century to another, and what they went through spiritually still spoke vividly to us in the twentieth century. This in fact is a theme going through sermon after sermon of his, and he never tired of repeating it. It influenced his evangelism very strongly, it permeated his theology when he came to know and appreciate the Puritans, it gave him a great love of revival history, and it made an impact on his theology of the Holy Spirit, especially when he read of the spiritual experiences of the Puritans.

All this lay ahead of him when he was still a schoolboy, but it was a classic case of the boy being father to the man. He kept up his reading—as I look around the shelves of my own library, I see many a volume of history that he urged me to read, or that he gave me as a Christmas present, or which, having read himself, he passed on to me to keep. Nor was his reading just Christian history—political history fascinated him too, and many of the books he gave me in later years were on Lloyd-George and the history of the first forty years of the twentieth century, a time through which he had grown up. He saw to it that his elder daughter Elizabeth listened to all the major wartime broadcasts that Churchill made, because she could then remember history in the making. His younger daughter Ann studied history at Oxford, as did I, and no one was more enthusiastic or supportive than the Doctor. His love of history also kept him in touch with the real world, with what was going on around him. This gave a powerful relevance to his evangelism, but also helped him pastorally as he could relate to those who came to see him.

The Calvinistic Methodists

Many people have asked the secret of his uniquely powerful preaching ministry. He might have had a first inkling of its roots as what we would now call a teenager, in 1913. That year he visited the Summer Association of Calvinistic Methodists, held in Llangeitho. To many the very idea of a Calvinistic Methodist might sound a contradiction in terms. Surely Calvin and Wesley were almost opposites? But the genius of the historic Welsh Calvinistic

Methodist Church was that it combined the very best of both. They had the fire, zeal and passion of the great eighteenth-century Methodist Revival. But they also had the powerful intellect and logic of Calvin's Reformed theology.

As we shall see later, Dr Lloyd-Jones was to define preaching very simply: 'logic on fire', or 'eloquent reason', or theology coming through a man who is afire spiritually. Much theology among modern-day evangelicals is either correct but dry, or impassioned but empty. The unique mix that made Dr Lloyd-Jones into the extraordinary preacher that he was comes from this background in Wales. He was both passionate and logical, emotional but always appealing to head as well as to heart, or, as he put it, logical and fiery.

In 1914 his father Henry Lloyd-Jones went bankrupt. For a while it looked as if the family would emigrate to Canada, in which case the history of British evangelicalism would have been very different. But, in God's providence, they moved instead to London where Henry set up a new business.

Coming to London

The early days were extremely discouraging. Young Martyn almost had to give up a very promising academic career and become a bank clerk in order to bring in some extra income for the family. Providentially, however, and to the loss of the financial world, trade picked up sufficiently at No. 7 Regency Street, and Martyn went on to gain a place at the well-known boys' school, St Marylebone Grammar School, near Harley Street. Martyn would in fact have made a good banker. He was always careful with his finances and never had any problems with debt, although as a pastor he never had much money.

When he died, he left a widow well provided for, and like many people who have known hard times, he was a model of generosity, a trait appreciated by both Christian organisations and young grandchildren alike.

Ironically, in view of his later career there, the Lloyd-Jones family decided not to attend Westminster Chapel when they came to London. They went instead to that great meeting place of Celtic exiles, the Welsh Chapel on Charing Cross Road. On their first Sunday there, they sat in front of some regular members of the congregation, the family of the eminent Harley Street eye surgeon, Tom Phillips. Bethan Phillips, the daughter, remembers noticing the three Lloyd-Jones brothers, little realising at the time how much one of them would one day change her life.

The minister of the Welsh Chapel was the Revd Peter Hughes-Griffiths. He was a strong character and an individualist, and like the young Martyn he had a passion for politics. Martyn at this time would often come home late, having spent the evening in the gallery of the House of Commons where he would watch his hero, David Lloyd-Jones—then Chancellor of the Exchequer in what proved to be the last ever Liberal Government—and others in debate. It was the high tide of the social gospel, the great 'nonconformist conscience', in which many a churchman preached more politics than anything else from his pulpit, and when a non-conformist clergyman still believed that politicians, especially those in the Liberal Party, could alter the world for the better.

The Great War of 1914–18 was, as we now know, to devastate all these hopes, and the Second World War, with all its horror, to destroy them completely. It instilled in young Martyn a lifelong distrust of what legislation could do to change things. It was the gospel, and the transformation which that brought alone, that could really change things. Not even the Puritans, whom he esteemed so highly, had been able to change people from within, the only change that could count. Puritan England had been succeeded by the immorality of the Stuart Restoration, because however much the godly had tried, the hearts of the people remained unregenerate.

Soon, therefore, young Martyn's hopes were to be dashed. But his father retained his liberal theology, something that many years later was greatly to grieve his son. Half a century afterwards, an American theologian asked him if his father had been a Christian. He did not know how to respond.

The Bart's man

For some time now, Martyn had one real interest—to study medicine and to become a doctor. 'I was never an adolescent,' he used to say, and at the age of only sixteen (much younger than usual) he entered the medical school of St Bartholomew's Hospital in London, universally known as Bart's.

Bart's had an internationally high reputation. So clever and knowledgeable were the young trainee doctors and surgeons said to be that there was a popular saying at the time: 'You can always tell a Bart's man, but you can't tell him much.' Certainly the young students believed that they were the best. In later years, the Doctor was to be offered honorary degrees and even the CBE from the Queen. He turned all of them down. To him, there was no greater award than to have the MD degree of London University.

Many of his contemporaries were to go on to glittering careers. One of them was Geoffrey Keynes, brother of the famous economist, John Maynard Keynes. Sir Geoffrey, as he later became, ended up as one of Britain's most eminent surgeons, as well as an international authority on the

poet William Blake. Another contemporary was the emin-
ent physician Arnold Stott—later Sir Arnold—whose son
John was to have such close links with Martyn Lloyd-
Jones in the future.

The calibre of these people shows how well Martyn
would likely have done if he had remained in medicine,
especially when you consider that his teacher was none
other than the royal family's physician Sir Thomas (later
Lord) Horder.

Dr Lloyd-Jones was to describe Horder as being 'the
most acute thinker that I ever knew'. He was someone
who taught his pupils by what is called the 'Socratic
method', which involves finding out the truth by asking
the right questions. Never just look at the symptoms,
which can be misleading—always probe deeper. He gave
Martyn, his star pupil, his own copy of Jevon's famous
scientific treatise 'The Principles of Science: A Treatise on
Logical and Scientific Method'.

This was to have a profound impact on the way in
which Martyn Lloyd-Jones thought—indeed it altered
his outlook for the rest of his life. He would always ask
behind the situation, probing here and there to see what
the matter *really* was, as opposed to what the person
thought it was. Someone would go to him and say,
'Doctor, I am feeling spiritually depressed.' To that person's astonishment, the Doctor would reply, 'Well, when
did you last have a holiday?' For the two things were not
as unconnected as people might think. When we are tired
and exhausted, life becomes grim and we see everything
through a prism of fatigue. This in turn reflects on our
spiritual lives: our prayers falter, not because we are
ungodly, but because we are too drained to stay awake!
Sometimes, too, depression of what seems to be a spiritual kind is actually physiological—we are medically ill

and need a cure. The difference that his medical training made to his pastoral ministry was therefore invaluable.

Much of the logic that later 'caught fire' came from what he learned under Horder. This can above all be seen in his evangelism. What was wrong with the world? Was it education? Well, the Second World War, fought between highly-educated countries, showed the folly of that idea. Other humanistic ideas would be examined, and revealed to be only the symptoms of the problem. No, the answer was that we were in sin, each one of us—in rebellion against God. What was the remedy? It was to be reconciled to God through his Son Jesus Christ on the cross. The diagnostic approach can be seen to full effect in the sermon he preached just after President Kennedy's assassination (which appears in *The Cross*). One human had tried, but failed, whereas another man who died young was now on the throne in heaven, the only hope for a lost humanity.

As will be seen, the Doctor continued to practise medicine informally long after he gave it up officially—often he was a better physician than the local doctor! His interest in medicine was lifelong. One of his great pleasures was to read the *British Medical Journal* for relaxation—we would jokingly refer to it as his comic! This actually helped me a lot once as a teenager. I had suffered a severe eye injury and was in St Thomas's Hospital. I developed some serious symptoms that the staff attributed to hysteria and therefore told me to pull myself together. However, my grandfather, on hearing the exact nature of the convulsions, became suspicious. He then remembered that they happened to a small percentage of patients who had been given a particular post-operative drug, about which he had read in the *BMJ* not long before. Most people took to the drug all right, but a few had exactly the kind of allergic reaction that I appeared to have as well. Being a doctor he was able to gain access to my surgeon, whom he knew, and the drug in question duly appeared in my notes as having been prescribed to me. With great glee, he informed us that the problem was solved. He was right—I was taken off the drug and never had the convulsions again.

This shows us two things. First, we see his great attention to detail. Secondly, as his daughter Elizabeth has said, it demonstrates 'his constant teaching that there are certain things you need to eliminate before you arrive at a diagnosis'.

His medical career blossomed. He had already started his general training at a much younger age than normal, and the momentum was continued. In 1921, at the unusually young age of twenty-one, he obtained his Bachelor of Medicine and of Surgery, doing so with distinction, and not long after that he went on to gain his Membership of the Royal College of Physicians and his Doctorate of Medicine. From now on, he was Dr Lloyd-Jones. The same year, following an especially brilliant piece of diagnosis, he was made Horder's junior physician, and two years later, still only twenty-three years old, he was given the key post of Horder's Chief Clinical Assistant. In 1924 he was given a major scholarship to study bacterial endocarditis, although he never went on to become a heart specialist as such.

Death, sadness and a change in direction

Although the glittering prizes were coming effortlessly in his direction, Martyn was not fully happy. Life was transient to him, and somehow empty. He had been greatly sorrowed by the early death in the 1918 flu epidemic of his much loved older brother, Harold, a budding poet who had been weakened through the deprivations he had suffered as a soldier in the war. Harold's death was romantic yet also futile. Their mother, a rather dominant and possessive woman, never really liked her sons' very natural interest in the fair sex. Harold, whom many regarded as a handsome man, had fallen in love. (As we shall see, Martyn had too.) His mother was duly awkward and Harold had had to go out in the cold to post a secret love letter to the young lady. This had the effect of weakening him fatally, and he died in the Spanish influenza epidemic, still in his early twenties, a waste of what could have been an outstanding life. He left his desk with a bookshelf, a 'secretary', to his brother Martyn, who in turn gave it to me. It is now in my library, and contains my copies of all the books written by my grandfather, of which Harold would have been proud.

Their father's death at a good old age was also a tragic blow—a gentle, scholarly man who was a deep inspiration to all his sons.

Many of Horder's patients were among the leading lights of their day—politicians, aristocrats and others, in addition to the royal family. But their notes were a revelation, as the dissipated lives they led became all too apparent. One immensely eminent personage died of what was probably syphilis—not that the ordinary people of the time knew it. The Prime Minister himself had a mistress in Downing Street. The other medical students wanted to gamble—though here Martyn was able to persuade them that they could enjoy playing cards more if they didn't have money at stake. But life was not as it should be and he knew it.

Although he excelled at medicine he began to feel another call—the 'hound of heaven' was after him. As we shall see in the next chapter, the Holy Spirit was working in him in a powerful way, both to convert him and to take him well away from Harley Street. But none of his medical training was wasted, and as is now clear, had he not become a physician first, his later career would never have had the power that it did. Having been a medical doctor, he was now to be 'the Doctor' for Christians—first in his native Wales, and then the world over.

2

Love and Marriage
1927

Psychologists do say that there are some key 'life changes' best not combined. These include things like changing jobs, moving house and getting married. In 1927 Martyn Lloyd-Jones did all three!

Let us start with the last of these: his marriage in January 1927 to Bethan Phillips, a match that lasted fifty-four years and which was lyrically happy.

To start with, it looked highly unlikely that such a union would ever take place, especially when the two first met thirteen years earlier. Bethan, born in May 1898, was nearly two years older than Martyn, and while they did not have teenagers as such in those days, differences in maturity were still marked, with girls normally maturing mentally and emotionally at a younger age than boys.

For Martyn it was almost love at first sight—indeed he truly loved no other woman than Bethan. For Bethan, to begin with, it was different—Martyn was so immature! It was not that she disliked him. It was simply that he was too young for her to contemplate returning the kind of affection that he very evidently had for her. The other thing was that as she grew older she became ever more striking in looks. She had the kind of physical features, especially the shape of her eyes, that in the 1920s were regarded as the height of beauty. Such looks never went to

her head—she was far too down to earth for that sort of
nonsense.

As a result she was sought by a lot of young men, some
of whom were immensely eligible. Through her father's
eminent position as an eye specialist in London, and
through the fact that the then Prime Minister David
Lloyd-George was Welsh, Bethan knew people in very
elevated circles, from 10 Downing Street onwards! Some
of these were bachelors, and the scion of one titled family
was known to be decidedly interested. She was often the
guest at fashionable house parties in the country, and
similar events. Such, of course, was not the Lloyd-Jones
style, and with little money, they had no possibility either.

In those days, dating was unknown, so a young man
would often simply propose to the young lady of his
dreams. Years later this became a kind of family joke.
'Didn't you have twenty-nine proposals of marriage?'
one of us asked her. 'Nonsense,' she replied, slightly
embarrassed, 'it was only twenty-seven. . . .'

One of those who did propose early on was none other
than her youthful admirer, Martyn. Things were slightly
different now, in that he had become good friends with
her older brother Ieaun (*pron.* Yiyan), who was training
for the ministry in South Wales. But still she said 'no'.
Martyn however did not give up. Various other possibilities appeared on the horizon—there was a young lady at
the hospital who was not without interest. But he spurned
all others. There was only one woman he loved, and she
was Bethan Phillips.

Martyn, alas, was not particularly good looking, and
was rather thin, and only too conscious of all those
eligible young men around. . . . To make matters worse,
he hated tennis—and Bethan loved it. Much courtship
took place in the 1920s upon the tennis court, and it is
a sign of Martyn's deep love for Bethan that he did his

best to learn it, albeit without much success. He also loathed dogs, while animals were deeply appreciated in the Phillips household. There were few things that he disliked more than being leapt upon by one of their huge dogs and being pinned to the chair!

Bethan was by now a medical student at University College Hospital. She was one of the early generations of women to study there. As time passed she found that she did enjoy Martyn's company. In fact, as friends, she enjoyed him a lot. And, as the years went by, that maturity gap disappeared.

She was now a single woman in her late twenties, which was much older than was the norm. With this came wisdom too, and an appreciation of what really mattered in life. When it came to that, Martyn had the true qualities, the ones that would last. So at last romance blossomed, engagement followed, and on 8th January 1927 they married.

It was, as it should be, a marriage made in heaven. She was the perfect partner for him in what God had planned for him to do. It has been said that Edith Schaeffer was the secret of L'Abri. Francis could never have gone for walks in the countryside, discussing philosophy with its futility with some seeking young person, had he not had a highly intelligent yet very practical wife who, when seeing a coach-load of backpackers coming up the mountain, was able to give them all lunch without so much as a flicker of hesitation.

With Martyn and Bethan Lloyd-Jones, it may not have been as stark a contrast as that, but without Bethan's strong matching qualities, Martyn could never have been the man he was. She used to say that it was her job 'to keep him in the pulpit'. This she certainly did, but not in the way many a traditional wife has done. She would, in public, always 'keep her place' as she saw it.

But she was emphatically never a doormat. As children, we were once asked who was the dominant person in the home in our parents' marriage. This we found hard to answer, and we had to conclude that each parent was evenly influential. But when it came to our grandparents, there was no question. It was 'Gu'—our grandmother! (Gu being the Welsh diminutive term of affection we used for her.) There was complete certainty in our minds that she ran the Lloyd-Jones household, and indeed she did. She did so with much love and care—she was no martinet. Her sense of humour was far too strong for that anyway.

But the main reason was that she needed to. Both the Lloyd-Jones brothers were, when it came to the practical side of life, as impractical as they were intellectually able—and they were two exceptionally gifted men. (Once, as a child, I received a school book prize on a really boring subject. My grandfather consoled me. Once, as a child, he had had a worse fate—a book on carpentry!) Martyn's physical speed of reaction was in inverse proportion to the rapier-like thrust of his intellect. We remember our grandmother so often crying out, 'Come on, Jones!' as he pondered slowly along, his mind on higher things, holding her up.

With her as a completely devoted and supporting wife, such things did not matter. He could have the time to prepare sermons, to change people's lives and later on to edit books. She enabled him to concentrate on what he was good at, while she looked after the rest. She realised that not everyone should be expected to have physical skills anyway. (How many men who can fix a broken pipe or mend a car engine have had the extraordinary impact of a Martyn Lloyd-Jones?) Unlike some women, she never despised her husband for what he could not do, and in no small measure this was not just a natural love of a wife for a husband, but a great admiration for the many things in life he did achieve.

Another reason that she was no doormat is that she had a strong intellect of her own, for which he was very grateful. He was never threatened, as some men are, by a woman who was not only strong willed but also mentally able. In fact his father-in-law Tom Phillips had prepared the way. Exceptionally for this time, his daughter was every bit as well-educated as his two sons. Bethan attended the North London Collegiate School which, then as now, was one of the best secondary schools for girls in the country. On top of that she was then university educated, at London University, and at University College in particular (which Vincent Lloyd-Jones also attended before going on to Oxford for a second degree).

University College was one of the first educational institutions in England which one did not have to be an Anglican to attend—a requirement not abolished until the 1870s—and it was therefore attended by many from Free Church homes like the Phillipses. It was also one of the best educational establishments in the country, and, being innately progressive, was one of the first to admit women as equal to men—the first Oxford or Cambridge Colleges to go 'co-ed' were not until the 1970s, though women were admitted to the universities themselves from the end of the nineteenth century. The Lloyd-Jones marriage was thus, rarely for those days, a marriage of two graduates of the same university.

So Martyn took his wife's mind seriously, not just her beauty! She was never as innately theological as he was. But she was one of the best critics of his sermons—something that would sometimes cause much amusement in the family, as she would say what she really thought of a sermon! Her criticism was of the best kind: completely honest, but given in the context of utter loyalty and deepest love. Furthermore, while his was the better theological brain, her knowledge of the Old Testament was unrivalled and far superior to his. We often felt that he had no need of a concordance—he had only to ask his wife! She would amaze us with the depth of her knowledge, knowing the most obscure passages and with an ability to remember the most complicated and unpronounceable names.

One interest they shared was their mutual love of the Welsh countryside—it was unsurpassed. When it came to music, however, their interests diverged. Martyn loved opera, but to Bethan it was all noise! He had to wait until his two daughters came along to have people in the family who shared his love of operatic music. (His nephew David Lloyd-Jones was later to go on to become a world authority on Russian music and Director of English National Opera North—opera was very much a Lloyd-Jones family interest.)

As we will see, she was also very wise when it came to people, and he depended on her very strongly for her assessments of them. Sometimes his enthusiasm would blind him to an individual's defects, whereas she would see through them straightaway. On some people she could be very outspoken in the privacy of the family!

He was able to help her too. Her family had a strongly developed sense of imagination—the 'Phillips imagination' we used to call it, because it was and has remained a very strong gene! When she lived near the sea after they married, she always feared that some great tidal wave would hit the town and they would all drown. (There is in fact an unusually good photo of her, taken at this time. One would never guess what was going on in her mind by looking at it!) When I used to visit Christians in Communist countries, the same 'Phillips imagination' would grip. I would fear imminent arrest on the border by the Secret Police before I ever reached my destination!

But of course such fears find no support in Scripture, however they are formed. (Some felt they were genetic; some took the view that they were learned from family behaviour traits.) However much one might fear, the truth is that Christians have a loving heavenly Father looking after them. Often we let our feelings dominate our lives, and these can paralyse us. This, with his medical training, apart from anything else, is something which Martyn fully understood. This is what makes his classic book *Spiritual Depression* so helpful.

— However much we might fear, we can also know the truth, and that knowledge, while not always removing the fear itself, can put it into a context which can help us fight what have been described by one pastor as our 'funny fears', the kind that we are sometimes too embarrassed to admit that we have, but which, of course, we can reveal to our spouse in the security of a happy marriage of the kind that Martyn and Bethan enjoyed. Even so, she never liked to tell him of her sea phobia when they lived in Aberavon, lest it distract him from his sermons! The advice given in *Spiritual Depression* is not only theological—remember who we are and how much God loves us because of the price at which our redemption was bought—but also practical: talk to yourself, remind yourself of these truths, do not let your feelings paralyse you. To those of us with the 'Phillips imagination', which category of course included his wife, this was the most wonderfully liberating news.

There was one other way in which Martyn was able to transform his wife's life, though if one believes as one should in divine sovereignty one would have to say that Martyn was the instrument that the Lord used. It is something that might startle us, but it was indeed true.

It was the fact that when Martyn married, he was a Christian but his wife Bethan was not.

That is to put it more dramatically than it appeared at the time—indeed if one had asked them that happy January morning whether this was true they would both have denied it, and quite sincerely.

But the truth is that Martyn was still emerging from a fog; from a theologically liberal background where the edges had been blurred. As we will see in the next chapter, he had wrestled long with the call to Christian ministry, but also with what being a believing Christian actually meant. By the time he married, he had reached the truth himself. But it simply never occurred to him that the wonderful woman whom he had just married could be anything other than a Christian like himself.

Indeed, if one looks at Bethan's background, one can see why, because no one could have come from a godlier family than she did. Her grandfather Evan Phillips was one of the most outstanding Christians ever to come from Wales—certainly, he could be described as the Welsh spiritual giant of the nineteenth century as his now grandson-in-law was of the twentieth. For Evan Phillips was very actively involved in not just one revival but two; not merely the more well-known revival of 1904–5, but also that of 1859, which was in fact more international than the later one, and with consequently greater effects spiritually.

(This greatly impressed itself on the Doctor, as we shall see, with one of his finest books being called simply *Revival* and based on sermons preached for the Centenary of the revival in 1959. As Iain Murray has also pointed out, the Doctor's theology of revival much influenced his better-known theology of the baptism with the Holy Spirit.)

Evan Phillips was a kindly man, but hated being

photographed. We had one likeness of him at home, in which he looked immensely stern. It had a profound effect on us, his descendants, as children. When it was placed in the playroom, we always felt that we had to behave in his presence!

He was quite a patriarch, surrounded by a large and loving family. He was for many years the minister of a church in Newcastle Emlyn, one that saw quite extraordinary things happen in the 1904 revival. His whole family knew one of its leaders, Evan Roberts, well—in fact Evan's son John taught him at one stage. From the Phillips home, 'Sunnyside', we had a cupboard in our house in Balsham, and Dr Lloyd-Jones used to sit next to it whenever he had a meal in our house. We often used to think as children, and indeed later, 'If only we could interview that cupboard! What tales it would tell!'

Tom Phillips (Bethan's father) was by 1904 in London, busy with his practice. But he knew from his family the quite amazing events of great spiritual blessing and outpouring that were taking place near their home and indeed in it. Travel to Wales was not as easy then as it is now. But he decided that while his two elder children— the third, Tomos John, had only just been born—might learn much in school, it would not matter if they missed class for a short while, because never again might they see a revival. So he packed off eight-year-old Ieuan and six-year-old Bethan, put them on a train and sent them to Newcastle Emlyn—and the revival!

Many, many years later, Bethan could not always remember where she had put her glasses, or what you had said to her not long before—although thankfully her basic mental faculties remained very much all there until she died aged nearly ninety-three. But she could still remember the revival as if it were yesterday, and well into her eighties she was able to pen an account for

Evangelicals Now, with total recall. She may not have understood all that she saw, but it never left her.

The sense of it never left her husband, either, although he never witnessed those events first hand. Decades later, when he decided where to be buried, he chose not to be with the Lloyd-Joneses and the Evanses, dearly though he loved his family. No, he wanted to be buried with his spiritual family, his in-laws, the Phillipses. So his grave is with theirs, just outside Newcastle Emlyn, where Evan Phillips preached, at Gelli cemetery, where his beloved Bethan now lies with him. (Rather touchingly, at her funeral, her recently born great-grand-daughter Myfanwy—the first great-great-great-grandchild of Evan Phillips—cooed as her great-grandmother Lloyd-Jones was interred. As one generation passed on, so another began.)

Bethan not a Christian, despite all this! Well, she realised this herself when she and Martyn went to Aberavon, though we are jumping ahead of ourselves in the story at this point. Bethan had never been a rebel, and so she had accepted much of what she had heard without really thinking how much it applied to her in the deepest sense. But listening to her husband's sermons, she realised that although she knew all about it, she did not have it in her own life. In a gentle way, she became a Christian through marriage to Martyn, and of course after that life was never truly the same, but even better still. They had not just each other, but a common Saviour too. Theirs was not just a happy marriage, but one to emulate, and for which to praise God.

3

The Aberavon Years

1927–1939

Into the ministry

As we have seen, although a more than promising career opened up before the newly qualified doctor, he never felt happy that this would be his lifelong work. He felt that 'the hound of heaven' was after him, calling him to a very different vocation—the preaching ministry. There was the disillusionment that we saw in the first chapter. But there was also a sense that the conventional, worldly answers to the problems of life were superficial, and that a very different kind of medicine was needed from the kind that he was giving his patients.

We can trace this change in the three talks he gave to the Literary and Debating Society of the Welsh Chapel in London. In 1921 it was on 'Modern Education'—a subject for which he retained a lifelong fascination. Then in 1924 it was on 'Signs of the Times'. This included an attack on modern fashions, including those worn by Bethan Phillips! But then in 1925 it was on 'The Tragedy of Modern Wales'.

By now the tone had changed considerably. He saw very clearly that the real tragedy of Wales was not that it lacked education, or indeed anything of that nature, but that it was *spiritually* hungry. The only real answer to Wales' problems was the gospel, a spiritual rebirth.

Considering the church in which he was preaching this, it was a brave talk to give. The Chapel was one of those which preached the social gospel, and which was close to the Liberal politicians of the day. When the talk became more widely known, it was seen as controversial. But it convinced him all the more that his real calling was to go to Wales and preach the only message that could save the country—the gospel itself.

His first sermon in Wales was in Pontypridd in April 1925. As in the Welsh Chapel, he preached a very different kind of message from the politically improving talk that was normal in South Wales. Social action was all very well, he thought, but what Wales needed was a 'great spiritual awakening'.

This in fact paralleled a great spiritual awakening of his own. It is impossible to pin down a date on which he was actually converted, as it seems to have been more of a process than a dramatic turn around at a particular moment. But whenever his own spiritual rebirth began, there is no doubt that the Christian message of salvation through Jesus Christ gripped him ever more and more, so that he felt his main calling in life was to proclaim it from the pulpit.

After his trip to Pontypridd, he postponed an immediate decision to go into the ministry. He still felt himself unworthy to be a minister, and decided to continue for the time being with his medical work, which was flourishing. But by 1926 the turmoil was over. As he himself said, it was 'God's hand that laid hold of me, and drew me out, and separated me to this work'.[1] He was called to be the minister of the Bethlehem Forward Movement Mission Church in Sandfields, Aberavon, and he accepted their offer.

The early years at Aberavon

Many years later, in his classic work *Preaching and Preachers*, he argued strongly that men should never enter the pulpit merely as a profession. Rather, they should only do so if they felt unable to do anything else and had been compelled by God's call into it. It helped, of course, if a man had natural talents as well—for example, a good speaking manner, a clear mind (though not, he would argue, necessarily an academic one) and above all, a fine character. But the main criterion was that such a man should be anointed by God for the task; someone filled with the Spirit, and with a passionate concern for the spiritually lost, and a deep pastoral concern for God's people. Such people did not call themselves—he rejected any such idea. Rather, they were men recognised by the church as being called by God. Preachers, he always said, were born and not made.

Nowadays, a young man having such a call would be despatched by his church to Bible college or theological seminary. The Doctor never went to such a place, and this is very important to understand if one is to comprehend the extraordinary ministry on which he was embarking. To the Doctor, a minister was not a technical expert, skilled in the knowledge of the finer points of Greek or Hebrew (though preachers always ought to be able to read the original) but primarily a preacher of God's word and a pastor with a divine commission. To be a preacher was to possess a gift from God himself, and too much academic learning could even be harmful. Wales was filled with preachers whose sermons might be academically respectable but which went over the heads of most of the folk in their congregations, and which were often theologically mistaken or pastorally disastrous.

So when fifty years later he and a group of friends set up

the London Theological Seminary, they went to considerable trouble to emphasise the essentially practical nature
of the course. To start with, there were to be no degrees
awarded. More important, the students were to be men
recognised by their local churches—who sponsored
them—as having the biblical gift of preaching, and the
lectures were to be given not by academics but by pastors
of churches skilled in particular areas, such as Greek,
Church History, etc.

Furthermore, as we have seen, it was his diagnostic skill
gained in medicine that made him the kind of preacher he
was, with his acutely analytical mind probing to find the
root of the problem.

In fact, when he first came in early 1927 with his newly-
wed wife Bethan, many of the local doctors felt alarmed!
Here was someone far better qualified than any of them.
In fact it was not until he solved an especially difficult
case with an unusually skilled piece of diagnosis that they
talked to him at all. Thereafter relations improved and
they were glad of his presence. A local chemist, Illtyd
Rees, had fallen ill, and the doctors were completely
stumped as to what the problem was or how to cure it.
Bethan had a strong feeling from God, which some may
nowadays describe as the biblical word of knowledge, that
the local doctors were going to ask Martyn to deal with
the case. To him, she was 'talking rubbish'. But in fact
two days later, the very summons came.

Before they had even arrived at the patient's house, Dr
Lloyd-Jones knew from a description of the symptoms
what was wrong with him. In his medical career he had
held the Baillie Research Scholarship, and the main object
of his research had been Hodgkin's disease, and a particular variant of it called Pell-Epstein disease. This man had
been showing precisely the symptoms of this illness. The
local physician was furious that the Doctor pronounced

on the illness that had so baffled them before he had even entered the house! But he agreed to go in, and examination proved his prediction to be exactly right.

This diagnosis greatly helped not just his relationships with local doctors, but also evangelistically, as it gave him a great reputation in the town. His elder daughter, Elizabeth, born in October 1927, remembers as a small child dozens of people visiting the manse, often with a medical problem.

With one case, it was not so much medical skill needed as detective work! In a place in South Wales, there was a girl who had been a nurse at his old hospital of Bart's, but who was now home with what seemed to be a very mysterious illness. Local doctors had theories as to what this disease could be, but were stumped for an accurate diagnosis. So Dr Lloyd-Jones was asked to investigate. It appeared that her evening temperature, always taken by her friend, another Bart's nurse, was very high, whereas when it was taken by others in the day time it was always low! This made the Doctor very suspicious, and he wondered whether she had not been happy at Bart's—her Matron there, whom he had known, was rather dragon-like! All was then revealed. As the Doctor had suspected, the girl and her friend had been expelled, as it turned out for the then serious offence of having men in their room at the hospital, and the illness was all a cover story. The Doctor agreed not to expose her story, but he was able to tell the local physician that she would now be making a total recovery!

One story of his medical time is rather touching. There was a man named Mort, who had had one major illness after another, involving numerous operations. The situation seemed hopeless. In this case, the Doctor was not able to do anything himself. But he was able to recommend a former colleague at Bart's, Sir Thomas Dunhill, who, as well as being a Consultant Surgeon there, was also Honorary Surgeon to the King. Sir Thomas was able to perform the operation, but to his amusement, just before the anaesthetic was due to be administered, he was told by Mr Mort not to stitch him up, but to use hooks and eyes instead, as he was bound to have to be opened up again soon! In fact the operation was a complete success, and Mr Mort was fully cured. Two years later, in fact, he had a baby boy, whom he named David Martyn Dunhill Mort!

The Doctor also came across cases of apparent mental illness. With one of them, he had described it in his own book on Romans 8: 5–17, *Sons of God*. A man had come to see him in a tremendously agitated state, and had just been discharged from a home, suffering it seemed from religious mania. He had been converted in the revival of 1904–5, but had since backslidden badly and become addicted to alcohol. He had suddenly realised his position, and had now convinced himself that there was no forgiveness. However, the Doctor was able to reason with him from Scripture, and he recovered completely.

Revival in Aberavon

However, it was not so much illness that was the problem in Aberavon and the surrounding areas, but spiritual blindness. Here the Doctor saw what in retrospect can only be seen as revival. It is this that gives what is almost a romance to his eleven years there from 1927 to 1938. Economically they were the hardest of times, as they were the years of the Great Depression, where unemployment was to be at its worst until the 1990s, but without the strong Welfare State provisions that were set up after World War Two to soften the blow. Things could not have been harder. Yet Aberavon was transformed in those years because of the powerful preaching of the message of Jesus Christ heard every Sunday at the Forward Movement Mission.

Some of this was of course the sense of expectancy of the preacher. As the Doctor said in a sermon in 1930, based on Jeremiah 17, 'Thank God, the age of miracles has not ended; the Holy Spirit is still abroad and one never knows when He shall descend upon us here at Aberavon. Let us be prepared!'[2] To many, the situation in Aberavon was hopeless, and humanly speaking that was an accurate statement. But the Doctor was one who believed powerfully in the sovereignty of God. Indeed, as one can see from his masterly sermons preached in later years on Ephesians and Romans, it was a deeply-held core belief. We cannot engineer revival, nor indeed could we ever convert anyone. But, as he told the congregation at Aberavon in his first year there, when asked, 'What can you do for such people?' his reply would be, 'Nothing! Absolutely nothing!' For 'in the affairs of the soul and the spirit no man can do anything for them, no matter how dear and how near he may be to them . . . no human being can do anything, but God can do everything'.[3] Indeed, as he made clear, again in his first year, in a sermon on 1 Samuel 17, 'St Paul did not convert a single person, he was but God's agent.'

As he said to them in his second year at Aberavon in 1928, in a sermon on 1 Thessalonians 1: 5:

Paul knew while he was peaching to them that something was happening. He knew he was being used of God, he knew the Holy Ghost was driving his words deep into their hearts and souls, he was conscious of that power which changes men and women and which had changed him. So he says that he preached 'with much assurance'. Of course he did! He knew he was *nothing* but the mouth-piece and the channel. God grant in His infinite mercy that it may be the same here tonight and that we all may experience that power and the blessed, gracious influence of the Holy Ghost! There is no greater joy which any minister may ever have than that, to know for certain that it is not he himself, but Christ in him, who is doing the work.[4]

In a very real way, that last sentence summarises the reason for the success of the ministry of Martyn Lloyd-Jones, not merely in Aberavon, but indeed throughout the rest of his entire life. It was what made it what it was—an abiding sense of the power of the Holy Spirit as part of a wider certainty of the sovereignty of God. As J. I. Packer has shown in his classic work, *Evangelism and the Sovereignty of God*, it is paradoxically those who believe most in the sovereign power of God who are and should be the best evangelists. It is because those who have this belief have such an expectancy, such an anticipation, that if the power of God is poured out on a place, the gospel will be irresistible and many souls will be saved.

This sense of God's power can be seen in the things the Doctor did from his earliest days—or, to some extent, in what he did not do! To start off with, he scrapped a lot of the social functions of the church, many of which had no doubt been established to win people into coming. Out went the sports club, the drama group and the temperance league. As he himself put it, 'The business of preaching is not to entertain, but to lead people to salvation, to teach them to find God.' Only preaching based on Scripture would do this, and he began as he meant to continue.

Little Elizabeth remembered even as a child the extraordinary sense that God was at work in Aberavon. She went to church all day on Sundays from the age of five, as did many of the other children. 'When I look back on it,' she recalls now, 'my awareness is of the presence of God . . . a sense of glory.' There was a 'radiant sense' in which even a child 'knew that God was there'. As she has said, 'They were great days.'

Few people in Aberavon were well educated. The Doctor had inherited a conviction from his father of the need to help working-class people. But unlike many middle-class ministers then and since, he believed strongly that working-class people were just as capable of listening to preaching as anyone else. There was no need to scrap the sermon. His style therefore reflected this. It was strongly expository, making clear to his congregation that the message of Jesus Christ was open to 'the very worst man in Aberavon'. That was as well, since the town had many contenders for that position!

Being strongly Welsh himself, he knew how easily his fellow country people could be stirred by emotion. Many preachers used this, of course, but it seldom had any truly lasting spiritual benefits. Being also a doctor, he felt that the 'medical approach' was the best. He would treat his hearers like patients, and this meant starting not with their easily swayed emotions, but with their heads. The mind had to be struck first.

So his message therefore was that Christian faith was 'very relevant and urgently important'. He broke all kinds of rules that we would regard as essential today. For example, he never cracked jokes, or used any kind of anecdote or personal story. Instead, he based himself solely and firmly on the message of the Bible. The gospel was truth, he preached, not 'based on experience' as were many false faiths, but 'on great eternal facts'.

Such methodology was to stay with him for the rest of his preaching career. (As a grandchild at Westminster Chapel, I was grateful that he stuck to his resolution never to refer to members of his family as illustrations during the sermon!) A well-known American preacher, John MacArthur, was greatly influenced by the Doctor's ministry. He once said how extraordinary it was that he could be accused of being biblical but not relevant in his Sunday sermons. If one was truly biblical, one was always relevant! To this, the Doctor would have given a loud amen. I have often seen this in editing his sermons for publication. What is continually impressive about them is that, for example, even if they were preached in the 1940s, over fifty years ago in some cases, they could in fact be preached in the 1990s, so profoundly relevant is their message. That timeless quality is something with which he began at Aberavon back in the 1920s and it has, of course, always been the great hallmark of true expository preaching.

It is indeed no coincidence that his very first sermon at Aberavon—preached in November 1926 just before he went there as pastor in 1927—was on the classic Pauline text, 'For I determined not to know anything among you save Jesus Christ and him crucified.' It is perhaps also fitting, and no coincidence, that those are the very same words that now appear on his tombstone in Wales.

The ministry in the church was soon growing. The whole congregation would meet every Wednesday to discuss practical living, while the men's 'Brotherhood Meeting' assembled for a more theologically orientated Bible class on Saturdays. The Doctor believed strongly that working-class men were every bit as capable of logical, biblical debate as those who were highly educated. Indeed, he would often argue that the men in his congregation, unskilled or unlettered as many of them were, often had a finer grasp of the great doctrines than did many professors of theology with numerous degrees.

His method of leading them was the Socratic method that he had learned on the hospital wards at Bart's under Lord Horder, learning through asking and answering questions. The best way to learn was to work something out for oneself. So he would ask the men and also the people who came on Wednesday nights, when one raised some point or other, to find reference to it in the Scripture. No other source was allowed. What did the selected passage actually say about something? How did it fit into the wider biblical context? Only then could the general principle be drawn out and applied to a person's life.

He would make people see the logic of their conclusions and, if necessary, point out to them where they were going wrong. He had, of course, a considerable knowledge of the Bible, and so was always able to remain in control of the discussions. Many of those who knew the Doctor, and were helped by him, were able to say that what often helped the most was that he was able to teach them how to think, and to do so biblically. This meant that when something arose in their life years later, when they no longer had him as their pastor, they were able to use the methodology of thinking through what the Scripture said about the problem and work out from that what they should do.

With preaching as distinctive as his, his reputation inevitably grew. In a Wales dominated by the social gospel and by liberal theology, his return to expository preaching and firmly biblical roots became noticed. Above all, he preached that people were sinners and in need of a Saviour. This was profoundly humbling, yet it reached out to and touched those who heard his uncompromising message.

As a secular journalist who heard him in Aberavon wrote at the time, there was 'no drama except for the great drama of salvation . . . Public emotion leaves him cold, yet his passion for human salvation sets his people on fire.'[5]

This was of course the 'logic on fire' by which, forty years later, he was to characterise biblical preaching, and which was the key to his own ministry. It was certainly having the most profound effects in the town. There were seventy converts in the church in 1929, his third full year there, and then 128 in 1930.

Often these converts were from the bottom of the social heap—the very kind of people whom Christians in the Western world are sadly so often failing to reach today. Not only were these folk saved, but their lives were completely transformed. The corporate life of the church was also an encouragement to them. All around them were people who had been converted who had suffered a life as hard as their own and could therefore understand them and help them. Many of the converts were local characters, such as the notorious drunk known as 'Staffordshire Bill'. He was converted and spent the rest of his life as a keen and active Christian. (Many of these stories have been turned into a book by Bethan Lloyd-Jones, entitled *Memories of Sandfields*. She never intended the stories to be a book, but when Iain Murray, the Doctor's official biographer, read them, he was so impressed that he put them into print.) Needless to say, the impact on the town of such conversions was tremendous, and did far more than any planned publicity campaign could ever do. Conversions are often the best witness to the gospel that there can be, and in Aberavon they had plenty.

Wider ministry

Inevitably, the Doctor's fame spread not just to other parts of Wales, but abroad as well. In 1932 he was asked to preach in Canada. His first sermon there was in Toronto, in the church of Dr Richard Roberts, a Calvinistic Methodist whose theology had sadly now become liberal.

However, the most prominent minister whom the

Doctor met in Toronto was the Revd T. T. Shields. The two men had much in common, as T. T. Shields was also a convinced Calvinist and an amillennialist as well. But despite that, the Doctor came to disagree with him, because he felt that Shields was far too polemical.

This is in fact significant, in view of the disagreements the Doctor was to have even with fellow Evangelicals over the issue of the doctrine of the church more than thirty years later. To the Doctor, Shields was someone who always disagreed with people, and was thus too negative. 'You can make mincemeat out of the liberals,' he told Shields, 'but still be in trouble in your own soul.' Rather than adopting Shields' divisive, antagonistic approach, the Doctor preferred to 'preach the Gospel to people positively and win them'. How one wishes that some of the Doctor's own self-proclaimed followers in our own day adopted such an approach!

For although the Doctor believed in what he did very deeply—and just how deeply we all knew as a family—he never believed in being publicly aggressive or harsh, however deep his private views might be. He would be zealous in his defence of the truth, but he did not believe in being *personally* aggressive. Indeed in later years, although he was to write a booklet against the ideas of the psychologist William Sargeant on the nature of conversion, the personal relationship between the two men was always good, as indeed it was with John Stott, with whose views on the nature of the church he strongly disagreed after 1966 (see Chapter 8 below). His attitude in 1932 was thus important, and a powerful indicator of how he meant to go on. As he once said, Paul did not hector Peter in Jerusalem, but won him over.

After Toronto, he went on to a conference organised by the Chautauqua Institute near Buffalo, in New York State. This gathering had sadly long lost any evangelical flavour that it might have had, and was the venue for speakers such as Eleanor Roosevelt and the leading humanist and scientist Sir Julian Huxley. But the Doctor felt that it was God who had caused him to be invited there, and the little-known preacher from South Wales found himself so popular that the small meeting room that he had been allocated had to be changed to the largest auditorium, where he was heard by over 6,000 people.

Beginning with student work

Of all the Christian activities with which Dr Lloyd-Jones was involved in his life, none has had such a worldwide impact as his work with students. As we will see later, his work with the International Fellowship of Evangelical Students (IFES) was to change the history of evangelicalism and make an impression that is still felt today.

This work, as so often, had a small beginning when, in 1935, he was asked to become involved with the Inter-Varsity Fellowship, now known in Britain as the UCCF (Universities and Colleges Christian Fellowship). This had been established eight years previously by a fellow former medical student, Dr Douglas Johnson, known affectionately over the years as 'DJ'. It had been established for Christians of all denominations—itself something of significance—in order to unify Christian student groups and unions in the different universities, colleges and medical schools. Douglas Johnson was now the General Secretary, and asked the Doctor to speak at its Annual Conference, because his 'Pauline' way of preaching had deeply impressed them.

Dr Lloyd-Jones was slightly hesitant at first, because he was a little unhappy about the rather English, hearty, 'public school' (the British equivalent of the American 'prep school'), anti-intellectual style then characteristic of IVF. But he finally relented, and so great was the impact he made, that in 1939 he was asked to be its President. This began a family connection. His son-in-law Fred Catherwood became President in later years, after serving for some while as the Chairman, and then his daughter Elizabeth Catherwood also became President, where she was deeply appreciated by both the staff and the students as a grandmother figure to whom they could tell the things on their hearts.

In the 1930s evangelical students were often in a minority, cowed by the larger and far more socially respectable, but strongly liberal Student Christian Movement (SCM). As a result of this, Evangelicals had retreated into a shell, or, to use a phrase later in vogue, into an evangelical rabbit hole. This meant that the students tended to concentrate on experience, rather than doctrine which was seen as too intellectual and thus frightening. As opposed to the strongly biblical worldview of the Puritans, which emphasised both the heart and the head, they leaned towards 'muscular Christianity', where getting into the Cricket First XI was more important than getting a first-class honours degree, and where any kind of intellectual debate with non-Christians was avoided. Consequently, the kind of Christianity practised by the evangelical students was rather flabby and lacking the solid doctrinal base of a biblically-rooted faith.

Nowadays, we take it for granted that we should use our head and think through the Christian implications of the world around us. But that is because of the legacy left to us by men such as Martyn Lloyd-Jones, which began with the work among students with the IVF. The Doctor, with his robust Welsh background and his strong emphasis on the importance of the mind, completely rejected their loose thinking. But instead of denouncing

it from the outside, he joined it and completely transformed it from within. He breathed a much needed air of
confidence into the IVF, and nowadays the roles on cam-
puses are reversed, as the InterVarsity in Britain group is
almost invariably bigger than any other Christian organisation, and SCM groups, if they exist, are usually tiny.

He achieved this by giving it the solid doctrinal foundation in the Scriptures that it had lacked. He taught
students first that they should be unafraid to think, in
private and in public, and then how they should think—
rather as he had done with the men's group in Aberavon.
He coaxed them from the rabbit hole environment by
showing them that they could relate their faith to their
studies—they had God-given minds and those minds
could be applied to their disciplines without their faith
being in any way sullied.

Although a medical graduate, he enabled arts and
literature students to feel that what they were studying
was perfectly appropriate, so long as they kept to their
faith and did not let the often worldly view of the artists
or authors they studied do them harm. There was nothing
wrong in studying a non-Christian poet, for example; nor
did they have to give their testimony whenever they wrote
an essay on one!

This was soon to be of great help to his daughter
Elizabeth, when she went up to study English Literature
at Oxford just after the war. Even then, studying English
rather than something 'useful' like medicine was frowned
upon in evangelical circles—a view for which the Doctor
had no time. My mother was taught by the great Dame
Helen Gardner (and also by C. S. Lewis, whose lectures
were packed). When my mother was studying Chaucer,
she had to write an essay on *The Miller's Tale*, one that is
distinctly bawdy in places. She therefore wrote a stern
essay for her tutor, telling her firmly that the Tale was

not seemly! Needless to say, this did not go down well with Helen Gardner, who had been expecting a literary critique.

Elizabeth then rang her father, and they agreed to discuss it in more depth when she came home from university at the end of term. The Doctor talked about it with her when the holidays began. 'He taught me,' she recalls, 'how to handle literature. Why,' he asked her, 'is the man doing this?' What was the author's aim? 'He taught me to look at it critically,' she remembers, 'not emotionally.' He also taught her 'to analyse a thing properly'. How well, for example, did Chaucer tell the story? Was he a good writer? If so, why? If not, why not? and so on. By all means *then* add a word about the morals of the author, but do so after having looked at it as literature first.

In other words, her father, although trained as a doctor, 'gave me a good lesson on literary criticism'. This was not surprising, of course. As his daughter has said, 'He was just terribly wise.' As a result, though, his daughter was in a stronger position, because she had been taught to think—something that she could apply in all fields of life thereafter, not just Chaucer. He was able, with Elizabeth, to do this one to one, but he did it in his speaking, and later in his writing, for whole generations of students.

Likewise, when I went up to Oxford to read modern history, he was always interested in the intellectual background against which the subject was being taught. He read, and later passed on to me, the works of the political philosopher Sir Isaiah Berlin, who was a professor at the University. He also enjoyed the works of the controversial historian A. J. P. Taylor, whose lectures one of my tutors told me to avoid! But my grandfather found them fascinating. The first one of his I read was in fact long before going to university, and was a book on the First World

War—one that my grandfather asked for from me as a Christmas present when I was a child.

The Master of my college, Balliol, was an outstanding historian, Christopher Hill. Hill was then and is still one of the leading authorities in the world on the Puritans, and his books were naturally of enormous interest to the Doctor, who either read them avidly himself, or read reviews of them in learned journals. But what makes Hill so fascinating is that despite his deep understanding of Puritan spirituality (I well remember the large numbers of Banner of Truth books on the shelves in his study) he was not only a non-Christian himself, but also a Marxist, albeit one of the many who left the Communist Party after 1956. Many Evangelicals would never be seen reading a Marxist author! Yet both the Doctor and I gained much from his work.

Indeed all too often we as Evangelicals fail to read those with whom we disagree. Sometimes this is because we feel it is pointless, yet as Francis Schaeffer and others, as well as the Doctor, have shown, if we are to understand the world around us and evangelise it effectively, we must at least know what people are saying. (The sermon reproduced in the *Evangelical Magazine of Wales*, in which the Doctor uses a review of a novel by V. S. Naipaul, is a brilliant example of how the Doctor was able to use the same methodology as that of the Apostle Paul on Mars Hill, by using the writings of non-Christians to show how we need the gospel.) But often too we are afraid that we will somehow be contaminated by the world—as some have put it, in rather alarming terms, those who 'go deeper always lose the faith'. The Doctor was able to show the sheer fallacy of this view. Indeed, to come into contact with Marxism or the like can in fact reinforce one's faith. As Schaeffer once put it, God's truth is 'true truth'—only the Bible has the real truth, the true outlook on the world. From some Marxists we could, as with Christopher Hill, learn much. But as the Doctor showed in his evangelistic sermons, there was an ultimate futility in all those who rejected the gospel; a futility that is tragic when a good man dies without the hope and life-giving freedom that only Jesus can give.

Another way in which the Doctor was able to help at the time was in introducing the idea of proper emotions— again, something which the English Puritans possessed, with their talk of 'experimental' faith—integrated with the mind. Too much IVF faith was dominated by the 'stiff upper lip' caricature of the English public school ethos. The Doctor, being Welsh, had in any case a Welshman's distrust of the English upper classes. But theologically he found their dislike of the intellect positively harmful spiritually, and he fought hard against it. The idea too of the gifted amateur—so vividly portrayed years later in the film *Chariots of Fire*—was one that he found equally pernicious. He also rejected the idea that somehow to go into 'full-time Christian work' was a higher calling. It was as Christian to be a good solicitor or factory worker as it was to be a church minister or medical missionary. This again was a strongly Puritan emphasis, rooted in the Pauline epistles.

By reintroducing the English Puritan emphasis back into British evangelical life, the Doctor thereby did it a huge service. It was of course 'logic on fire' again—you used your brain (logic) and let it change your life completely (fire). As a result, British evangelicalism after the war was a very different thing from what it had been before.

Back to London

Martyn Lloyd-Jones' fame in Wales continued to spread, because of the great work that God was doing through him. The secular press was by now describing him as the greatest preacher in Wales since the revival of 1904. But as he rightly pointed out to the 7,000 or so who came to hear him at the Daniel Rowlands Centenary Meeting in 1935, Wales had forgotten the truths upon which the revivals were based. People were still living off the fat of the revival, even though it had now taken place over thirty years ago. This produced a very backward-looking Christianity which sadly still affects Christian life in Wales today.

Indeed, he told a packed Albert Hall the same year that revival could not be artificially induced. Revival is something sent sovereignly by God. (One can read this in the two books in which he talks most about the subject— *Revival* and *Joy Unspeakable*—where he provides a clear biblical exegesis of the subject.) Evangelism, he told them then, as he was to say many times again in subsequent years, had become too obsessed with results, and decisionism was no substitute for the proclamation of the truth in all its fullness.

In 1937 he went again to the USA, and preached in Philadelphia. One of his listeners was Dr Campbell Morgan, once more minister of Westminster Chapel after a time abroad. He was deeply impressed with the sermon, and decided that he must ask Dr Lloyd-Jones to join him there.

For the time being, the Doctor declined, as he felt that God was still telling him to remain in South Wales. But later he felt that God was calling him to return to London and go to Westminster Chapel. Needless to say, the congregation in Sandfields were not happy with this decision.

But several remarkable 'coincidences' confirmed the decision. Earlier in 1938 (not long after the birth of their younger daughter Ann), he had been asked to become the minister of St Marylebone Presbyterian Church in

London—near his old school. He had refused because there was also the possibility of becoming Principal of the Calvinistic Methodist College in Bala, North Wales. While waiting for their decision on whether or not to invite him to the College, Dr Campbell Morgan asked him to fill in time by coming on a purely temporary basis to Westminster Chapel.

So in September 1938, he preached his first sermon at Westminster Chapel. Characteristically, the subject was on the importance of doctrine to the Christian life!

Then in December, the Chapel asked him to stay with them permanently, working alongside Morgan as joint minister. He refused this offer, as he was still uncertain as to what he was supposed to do next. But in 1939, his principal supporter at the College missed the train to the vital meeting to decide on the new Principal, and the College turned him down. Those present had disliked his strong and resolute stand on the gospel and his rejection of liberal theology.

Instead, the Lord had opened the door to the biggest Free Church in London; one which, under Campbell Morgan, had developed a world-renowned ministry. There was now not the slightest hesitation in Dr Lloyd-Jones' mind. He accepted the offer of Westminster Chapel and was to remain there for nearly thirty years. While some have regretted his choice to leave his native land, there is no doubt that he could never have had the extra-ordinary international ministry that he did had he remained in Wales. Furthermore, London was not just a large city, or even the British capital—in those days it was also the capital of the British Empire. London was at the hub, and it was for there that the Doctor, his wife Bethan and their two daughters, Elizabeth and Ann, now departed.

Wales never forgot him, of course—nor did he forget

Wales. Many of his holidays were taken there, and he preached all over Wales regularly, often in Welsh. As we will see later, his influence in Wales actually grew. He continued to be revered in Aberavon. I will never forget going down there in 1977, on the fiftieth anniversary of his appointment. The church was packed! Many of the people in the congregation remembered him from when they were younger, and the old church secretary, E. T. Rees, was still there.

In the evening he preached on the biblical description of the 'cloud of witnesses'. The old converts like Staffordshire Bill were, humanly speaking, long gone. But one could sense the presence of the cloud of witnesses there very strongly that night—it was as if they were looking down upon us, joining us in praising God for all the extraordinary things that had happened in Aberavon in those years. The feeling I got was as if the Doctor had left only yesterday. He had gone to London, where he had remained for nearly forty years, but he was always a Welshman.

4

Westminster Chapel
1939–1968

The Chapel during the war

Westminster Chapel and Dr Lloyd-Jones are synonymous
in the minds of thousands of people all over the world,
even though he was in fact only there for thirty of his
eighty-one years. But along with the work of IFES, it is in
many ways his most lasting legacy. This is all the more the
case with the Chapel because of the books that came out
both in his lifetime and after his death. Most of these are
edited transcripts of the sermons he preached there,
especially those after 1945.

Much has been written about Westminster Chapel
during those years. So what this chapter will do is examine the unique features that made the Chapel under the
Doctor the remarkable place that it was. It will then go
on to look at ministries not directly part of the Chapel,
but which took place there—notably the Westminster
Fraternal and the Puritan Conference.

During the war it was amazing that the Chapel survived
at all—in fact it survived a bomb exploding nearby, which
showered the Doctor with debris from the ceiling. It was
characteristic of him, his daughter Elizabeth recalls, that
not only did he remain absolutely calm, but after a few
minutes' pause—the noise had been deafening—he went
on with his prayer! He was preaching from Jude, and his

text suddenly became rather apposite—it was on 'building yourselves on your most holy faith'. He was able to show the congregation how sure a foundation we can have in the gospel of Jesus Christ—as opposed to the building literally falling apart around them!

My mother has many memories of going to church in wartime. Another flying bomb landed even nearer to the Chapel, and this made the fabric unsafe. The congregation had to go for a while to nearby Livingstone Hall. 'We were small in number,' Elizabeth Catherwood recalls,

> and the sense of danger from the unpredictable bombs was ever present. But our sense of fellowship was very strong, and though few in number and in somewhat depressing surroundings, we still knew the presence of the glory of the Lord. One evening my father had preached with great power on the man without the wedding garment. At the end of the service, a lady came to speak to him. She was one of three elderly sisters—the other two had come from the South to spend the weekend with her—and before leaving she said to my father with a radiant face, 'All is well with me, Doctor. I have my wedding garment.' That night all three sisters were killed by a flying bomb, and when my father told us the following week, we rejoiced that the Lord had taken the three sisters into his presence. But wise pastor that he was, he urged us to make sure that we too were ready.

Another great memory of wartime were the hundreds of visitors from the Allied forces. There were uniforms of all shapes and colours and there was a feeling of great warmth of belonging to Christian brothers and sisters from overseas. Many of them, especially those from occupied Europe, did not know how their own families were under Axis rule. As Elizabeth recalls, it was a foretaste of the longer-lasting fellowship—this time with Germans included—of the wonderful fellowship of the IFES, in which the Doctor was to play so crucial a role.

The Doctor was still joint minister with Dr Campbell Morgan until 1943. Then he became his own man, and the congregation at Westminster became very much that drawn together by the quite outstanding teaching ministry of Martyn Lloyd-Jones.

Many a mighty preacher lost impetus on coming to London. However, with the Doctor, impetus increased. The war years had naturally depleted much of the congregation, as it had been dangerous for those from outside London to travel into the centre. However, by 1947, only two years after the war ended, the morning congregation averaged around 1,500 a Sunday, and the evening service no fewer than 2,000.

It was of course the preaching that drew the people. One of the first things he did when able to act under his own authority was to scrap the choir. As one sees clearly in his book *Preaching and Preachers*, it was the proclamation of the word of God that was central. This flowed with his view of the sovereignty of God. There was no need for man-made thrills to entice people to the Chapel! Some of the old followers of Campbell Morgan adapted well to the new regime and stayed. Others left, leaving the Doctor with the kind of congregation who wanted what he gave.

We saw in the first chapter that the Doctor as a person embodied the style of preaching that he used at Westminster—'logic on fire'. We can look at it in more depth here, because it is the explanation, in the plan of God, that made the Chapel the phenomenon that it was in the twenty-five or more years during which the Doctor was at the height of his powers.

He defined preaching as 'theology coming through a man who is on fire', filled with the power of the Holy Spirit and called by God himself to proclaim it. He had the highest opinion of that calling. Preaching from

Scripture—biblical exposition—was to him nothing less than 'God's method'. His job as a preacher was not to give his own ideas—London was filled with preachers who did just that. Rather, he saw his task as making known God's message from God's word. The preacher never spoke with his own authority. Rather, it was an unction from God. This is why he felt that all preaching 'must be expository'—in other words, an exposition by the preacher of what the Bible was saying—because it could never really be anything else if it were to be the genuine article.

He himself was immersed in Scripture. I well remember him using the Murray McCheyne system. This involved reading four passages of Scripture a day—usually two in the morning and two at night. Usually, the Doctor would read from one of the evening passages when he was staying with us and leading family prayers. He knew that Bible inside out!

The Bible gave the total picture. This is why he used the method he did, going through verse by verse, because he needed to make sure that he got out everything that was there. In later years, he would often spend weeks on a verse, and it is for this that he has become known. However, in the 1940s and early 1950s he would normally not spend more than two Sundays on a verse, as one can see if one reads the John 17 series of sermons, or the quintet being published from his series on 1 John. He would compare scripture with scripture, so that people were capable of getting both the details and the whole panorama. This is where his knowledge of the *whole* Bible became so important. Furthermore, while he was never 'topical'—the idea to him was anathema—he was always relevant. As Chua Wee-Hian, a former attender at the Chapel and later General Secretary of the IFES, has put it: the Doctor, unlike so many other preachers, always gave people 'the whole message'.

J. I. Packer, then a student in London, has summarised the days there well. He called the Doctor's preaching in those years 'a plateau of supreme excellence',[6] which taught him all he needed to know about how it should be done. There is indeed a freshness about those sermons which, reading them half a century later, is quite remarkable. As Packer has written, the Doctor 'effectively proclaimed the greatness of God, and of Christ, and of the soul, and of eternity, and supremely of saving grace—the everlasting gospel, old yet ever new, familiar yet endlessly wonderful'.[7]

As Packer continues, in

> some way there was in the Doctor's preaching thunder and lightning that no tape or transcription ever did or could capture—power I mean, to mediate a realization of God's presence. . . . Nearly forty years on [Packer wrote this in 1985] it still seems to me that all I have ever known about preaching was given me in the winter of 1948–49, when I worshiped at Westminster Chapel with some regularity. Through the thunder and lightning, I felt and saw as never before the glory of Christ and of his gospel as modern man's only lifeline and learned by experience why historic Protestantism looks on preaching as the supreme means of grace and of communion with God.[8]

Furthermore, as Packer so rightly points out, the Doctor was also a great evangelist, making the emphasis of his Sunday evening sermons the need for salvation, with the morning sermons mainly aimed at nurturing Christians. It was in his evangelism, Packer feels, that the Doctor was

> as a communicator . . . at his finest. He was bold enough to believe that because inspired preaching changes individuals it can change the church and thereby change the world, and the

noble purpose of furthering such change was the whole of his life's agenda. As for force in pursuing his goal, the personal electricity of his pulpit communication was unique. All his energy went into his preaching: not only animal energy, of which he had a good deal, but also the God-given liveliness . . . called unction . . . the anointing of God's Holy Spirit upon the preacher.[9]

Graham Harrison, a fellow Welshman and close colleague, has written of the 'power of argument and logical progression as he unfolded his message in such a way that the simplest could follow him and the deepest could but marvel at his profundity'.[10] This was of course the logic learned from Lord Horder at Bart's, now used to wonderful spiritual effect in his preaching ministry back in London.

To the Doctor, the notion was ridiculous that said, as we now lived in an age of mass communication, people would be unable to follow logic and careful thought. Nor did the preacher need to know what individual struggles folk in the congregation were going through. Sin as sin, not specific problems, was what was wrong, and that was universally true.

Graham Harrison has also pointed out another key ingredient of what made the Doctor's Westminster Chapel so special. It was the sense of the glory of God— the feature that even little Elizabeth had noticed as a child at Aberavon. God was alive and at work, and the Doctor never failed to confront his listeners with this sense. As Harrison has written, this was not always a 'comfortable experience'[11] for those in the pew. But when he proclaimed the glory of God and the need for salvation, he always 'reasoned . . . as he preached'. He argued in 'big, bold, logical steps that were so compelling in their presentation of the truth'.[12] As John Stott, from 1950 the Rector of another big London church, All Souls, has put it, 'He combined the analytical prowess of a scientifically trained mind with the passion of a Welshman.'[13]

Much of this sense of the presence of God came from the seriousness with which he approached the task. He believed that what he was doing was far too important for humour, at least in the pulpit. His sombre, long, black Geneva gown only enhanced the effect. But when he began his long prayer, the whole atmosphere would change. One felt almost transported into the presence of heaven as he began. Out of the pulpit he was 'Dacu' to his grandchildren, our deeply beloved grandfather. In the pulpit it was as if he were someone else. We knew he was our grandfather, but such was the sense of God's presence with him that we could make the distinction between his two roles in our lives.

Jim Packer has described this well in *Chosen Vessels*. It is important to an appreciation of those extraordinary years. Packer writes:

> What a fascinating human being he was! Slightly built, with a great domed cranium, head thrust forward, a fighter's chin and a grim line to his mouth, he radiated resolution, determination and an unwillingness to wait for ever. A very strong man, you would say, and you would be right. . . . There was a touch of the old-fashioned about him: he wore linen collars [which, to my grandmother's despair, he could take for ever to put together] three piece suits, and boots in public.[14]

Indeed, as my mother vividly remembers as a child, he would wear *all* these clothes on the beach! While other fathers were in swimming trunks, playing cricket with their children, he would be in not only his suit, but also his hat, reading works of Puritan theology!

Packer continues that the Doctor

> led worship as worship was led a hundred years before his time. In the pulpit he was a lion, fierce on matters of

principle, austere in his gravity, able in his prime both to growl and roar as his argument required. Informally, however, he was a delightfully relaxed person, superb company, twinkling and witty to the last degree . . . He did not suffer fools gladly and had a hundred ways of deflating pomposity. Honest, diffident people, however, found in him a warmth and friendliness that amazed them.[15]

In other words, in a day in which warmth and camaraderie in the pulpit as well as outside it was supposed to be essential to win people, the Doctor broke all the man-made rules of success, and was enormously blessed by God in the process.

Another way in which he bucked the trend was the fact that although there were many converts at the Chapel, he never once made an altar call. He was completely against putting any kind of pressure on his hearers. 'Going for decisions' was a very alien concept to him, because it went against his view of the sovereign power of God. If God was working in someone, convicting them through the Holy Spirit of their need of salvation, anything that humans might do to apply pressure was purely superfluous! Our duty was to present the truth of the gospel, and God did the rest.

This was also partly why music was not such a priority at the Chapel as elsewhere. This was not to say that the Doctor personally had no time for it—far from it! My mother remembers going with my grandfather to the opera, for which he (if not she) had a particular love. This was shared with other members of the family. He greatly encouraged my own love of music when I was at school, and his nephew David Lloyd-Jones became Musical Director of English National Opera North. David always refers to his Uncle Martyn with the greatest warmth, and once told me, 'I loved him dearly.' Rather, he saw preaching as the central purpose of being at church—

gathering together to hear God's word. Music, as he points out in *Preaching and Preachers*, can have a tendency to dominate the service. He used to hate the experience of sitting through choirs that never seemed to stop, and which restricted the time he had to preach! Furthermore, people also used to use music as a means of getting folk into church, and of creating the right atmosphere. To him, God's word drew people, and the Holy Spirit could always be trusted to put the listener in the right frame of mind. There was no need for excitement when one had the Holy Spirit at work! Freedom in the spirit when he preached was, to him, the key to the whole thing, and one could therefore describe it properly as the secret of his success.

The congregation

One of the other things that made Westminster Chapel completely unique was the unusually varied range of the congregation. In fact that is a massive understatement! I well recall as a child folk from university professors through to mental patients, and everything in between! Going to the Chapel was certainly an unpredictable experience when it came to the people one would meet there.

In fact Westminster Chapel in those years throws the 'homogeneous unit principle' so beloved of church growth specialists utterly on its head. No group of people could have been less homogeneous, yet the sense of unity was extraordinary. There was a sense of expectancy, of hearing from God, of excitement at what the Bible was saying. It was of course the unity of the Scriptures themselves, for whom the dictums of modern sociology, helpful though they can be in some contexts, were unknown. The Doctor's preaching could be understood by everybody, which is why everybody came, often from considerable distances. Some were professional people. One of them was Quinlan Terry, now world famous as an architect and as one of Prince Charles' architectural advisers. But another one was a strange old lady whom we all knew by the unfortunate name of 'Mad Annie'; a lady under a permanent series of delusions, most of which involved her as being the daughter of some famous historical character! But insane though she may have been, she was one of the most faithful attenders of Westminster Chapel in those years.

Many of the congregation were from overseas. The Chinese were there in great numbers. Among them, as we have seen, was Chua Wee-Hian, now himself the minister of a church in London after leaving the IFES. Other former international students went on to hold key positions in the church worldwide, among them being Gottfried Osei-Mensah, who not only became a Vice-President of the IFES, but also Executive Secretary of the Lausanne Commission for World Evangelisation. Another former attender, Daniel Arap Moi, later became President of Kenya.

The Doctor's Welshness had much to do with this. Unlike others, he treated overseas visitors the same as anyone else, neither rejecting them nor being condescending towards them. Being Welsh, he knew what it was like to be under English oppression! And his dislike of the typically Anglo-Saxon denial of emotion meant that the international part of the congregation felt understood and appreciated by him, and they loved him for it. It was very much a foretaste of heaven to come as one saw folk from so many different cultures all coming together to worship God and hear his word.

It also helped his family—indeed that, and the ministry of IFES, completely changed it. It gave us a sense of God's bigness that would be impossible to learn otherwise. We would often have African students to lunch, for example, and talk easily to people who often found that the white world around them rejected them, while we did not. Seeing people with other skin colours became normal to us from an early age.

The Doctor did not neglect the pastoral side of the ministry, either. To many people, this is as much part of what they remember as the sermons on Sundays. As his congregation came from so far and wide, it was physically impossible for him to go out to see everyone. So they came to him, to his vestry, a room behind the pulpit. He always made sure that he was available to be seen after the service.

One such person, in late 1953, was a young accountant. The Doctor's sermon that night had been especially powerful, so he was distinctly nervous! Yet the lion in the pulpit turned into a lamb in the vestry, and gave permission for Fred Catherwood to marry his elder daughter Elizabeth.

Many of the conversations though were with people who were in agony of soul. Countless lives have been changed through time spent in the vestry with the Doctor. What was so unique about him, as we have seen, is that he was medically as well as spiritually qualified, and was able to strike a balance between the two.

He was also very kind to those who needed it. Ray Gaydon was a former South London 'rocker', a youth gang of the time, and a worker on a building site. He was converted and had started coming to Westminster Chapel. He also felt that the Doctor was a 'lion in the pulpit and a lamb in the vestry'. Ray later went on to become a teacher, then a Baptist pastor before going on to other things, including playing a key role in setting up the Martyn Lloyd-Jones Recordings Trust, the ministry which makes available the Doctor's sermon tapes.

But life at the Chapel was not just a matter of going to sermons. During the war, it was not safe to go home at lunchtime, so at my grandmother's suggestion, the kitchens were used so that people could stay on for lunch. This worked well, and the practice continued for the rest of the Doctor's ministry.

Elizabeth Catherwood has many happy memories of the full days spent at the Chapel. As she has said:

> We who spent all day Sunday were the Church family, the nucleus who under God supported the whole work. So we had our lunch, and talked, and fed strangers, and shared our thoughts and our problems. . . . My mother, who was very much at the centre of the time together, always wise, always a good listener, led the Women's Bible Class, talking, encouraging and advising. She was an able lieutenant to her husband, and dealt with many of the problems herself, but always referring to him those she felt needed his particular help. They were great days, and whenever some of us meet again, we always refer to them with gratitude.

This is one of the parts of life at the Chapel that I remember most. Everyone had their usual places for lunch, sitting near the same people, but everyone soon spoke to everyone else. Many families ate baked potatoes, and there was a large oven into which we would put them before the morning service. I have often been fascinated with heraldry, and maybe my interest began then. As there were so many potatoes from different families, each potato had to have a special mark on it to distinguish it from the others. Ours, I recall, had a noughts and crosses motif, surrounded by a large C.

Lunch, which took place after the morning service, was a time of fellowship. The Chapel has been criticised for not being a local church, and for lacking 'body life'. It was in a sense a local church only for those who enjoyed the superlative preaching, or local to those who lived in London and a 100-mile radius. (Some people came a long way!) So in that sense the church was not a local one. This begs the question whether a church should always be local, but this is not the place to discuss such weighty issues! Suffice it to say here that when the Doctor retired in 1968, many people from the Chapel did go to their local churches, and having had the benefit of years of the Doctor's teaching, were able to make an enormous difference to the spiritual lives of their local congregation.

However, in terms of 'body life' nothing could have been stronger than the Chapel! With most churches, the majority of people only see each other at services or at sparsely attended mid-week meetings, or at home group Bible studies. At Westminster Chapel, by contrast, we saw each other all day. Lunch did not fully fill the space between the morning service and the afternoon discussion classes, or Sunday school.

The Doctor's Catherwood grandchildren were still young during his ministry (when he retired we were thirteen, nine and seven years old) so we often went out to museums and other improving places. All of this helped to make Sunday fun. While there was no immediate spiritual benefit in going around an art gallery, it created a sense of liking Sunday, which is very important. How many young people are lost to church because Sunday is for them a day of total boredom?

Sunday school followed. This was not just for children, but for adults too. During my grandfather's time I was in the junior department. My father led a class, full of very vigorous discussion, for young people of both sexes in their twenties and thirties. There was also my grandmother's class for women—a few of whom attended it during the entire time she led it—and then a class for older men and for women who did not attend Mrs Lloyd-Jones' class.

For me, the next event was a special time. My grand-father would summon me into his vestry to write in the record book details of the subject of his text, and details of the Bible passage read, and the hymns. Historians looking at such things must have wondered why the hand-writing in the record book looked so childish. Well, it was just that! It was especially indulgent of the Chapel staff to allow this, as my handwriting was like my grandfather's in being not all that easy to read. But to the Doctor, it was a useful as well as pleasant way of spending time with his eldest grandchild; one who was, as we shall see, a Chris-tian for the last two years of that momentous ministry. To me it was not only a great honour, but also enormous fun, and I would occasionally be rewarded with a 'chocolate coin'—something that the other children in the church only received from him at Christmas.

Tea then followed. We usually sat at a different table for this. Those with children often went home then, so it was a huge privilege for me to be able to go to the evening services as it meant that I was truly grown up! Those not going home often went to the prayer meeting, which took place before the evening service. At night, the Doctor was normally evangelistic, although still firmly expository—one can read the sermons he preached in 1963, for example, in his later book *The Cross*. After that, there was coffee or tea in the hall at the back, and for those who had been there all day, they finally left after being in or near the Chapel for about ten hours. Quite a day!

But it was the kind of day that few ever forgot. Even after the Doctor had retired, and people went to their local churches and went home for a Sunday roast rather than baked potatoes at the Chapel, they always remem-bered not just the sermons at the Chapel, but also that unique sense of fellowship, and that distinct sense of the glory of God. I can remember it now, over twenty-five years later, even though I never knew the Chapel as an adult. We probably took it all for granted at the time, and it is with hindsight we can see what an enormous privilege it was to be there for such a special time. They were indeed, as the Doctor's elder daughter has said, 'special days'.

5

The Westminster Fraternal and the Puritan Conference

The Fraternal

When the Doctor was dying in 1981, he made one thing clear about his memorial service. He always felt himself to be the 'pastor's pastor', and as a result, the man who had been his right hand for many years, John Caiger, was to lead the service. It was in fact the only request he made concerning that event, and as a family we were happy to see that it was fulfilled. He wanted more to be remembered as the minister's minister, he told us, than he did even for his time at Westminster Chapel. In fact, as with his involvement with IFES, it was a work from which he never retired, and to which he was completely devoted. As he told John Caiger, his involvement with helping other ministers was 'one of the greatest privileges of my life'.

The origins of his role as pastor to pastors went back to a study group in 1941, at the request of Douglas Johnson of the IVF. But its real beginning, as a group of ministers, started in 1943. Much has been written about the Westminster Fellowship, and so what I write here is, as with the chapter on Westminster Chapel, designed to give more an impression of what made his role so special than a detailed description of different meetings.

It began as a group of ministers who met informally once a month in Westminster Chapel at lunchtime. By

1954, however, it had grown considerably and averaged around 200 ministers a month, becoming twice that size by the 1960s. It was very much a gathering for pastors rather than for just anyone who was interested, and for the first twenty-five years of its existence, it was open to any pastor who was an Evangelical, regardless of denomination. (This meant that Anglicans and others in 'mixed denominations' were welcome to attend, so long as they themselves were Evangelical.) The Doctor was the Chairman, and he was to keep this position right up to his death, leaving it only when it was clear that his life had not long to go. His thirty-eight-year tenure of the chair therefore took up over half his adult life, and he was to be involved with that post for longer than anything else he did.

Much of the rationale for the meetings was for pastors to be able to raise either problems or doctrinal issues from their own church. Needless to say, this meant that all discussions had to be on the basis of the very strictest confidence.

Hywel Jones, in his piece *The Pastor's Pastor*, has given a wonderful summary of what it was like to be a member. (I refer to some of the things he has written in the chapter '*Joy Unspeakable*'.) The Westminster Fellowship or the Fraternal, as the meeting came informally to be known, brought out the best in the Doctor. With his wonderfully incisive mind, he would get through to the basis of the problem. But it also brought out the loving pastor in him. Many of the members of that Fraternal became like sons to the Doctor, some becoming especially close over the years. (All of them often felt that they alone were the closest! We knew in the family that this was not true. With his close circle, he was devoted to all of them alike, as a father often is to children who are very different from each other but equally his children, all the same.)

The Doctor was always excited by the Fraternal, and would share this with his family. His daughter Elizabeth recalls:

My mother, Ann and I often used to enjoy hearing my father's accounts of the issues that had been raised at the ministers' fraternal. Of course he did not talk about the ministers' individual problems, but he was always stimulated by the day's discussions; he would talk about them with enthusiasm, and show how he had arrived at the conclusions. The subjects would have been many and various—the Revd Omri Jenkins reminded us at his memorial service that my father, one Monday, gave a lengthy and totally impromptu address on acupuncture! He loved those days and his pleasure in them overflowed throughout the evening afterwards.

Hywel Jones has described the Fraternal as the Doctor's 'finishing school for ministers'.[16] Finishing schools are supposed to make their pupils 'ready for life' and Jones writes:

So the Doctor sought to make those who had the irreplaceable privilege of being members of the Westminster Fellowship *ready for life*. . . . The meeting focussed on the reality that is the existence and nature of the spiritual as well as the physical world . . . Yet the Doctor saw to it that the pre-eminent position was given to the spiritual because, without that dimension, complete sense could neither be made of the physical nor could there be any solution to its problems.[17]

This was, of course, the same thing that he had always preached—that the basis of all our fundamental problems is spiritual.

The attenders at the Fraternal were a fairly widely-based bunch, and, as Jones comments, for

a meeting with such scope and aim extraordinary gifts were necessary, gifts not commonly found and certainly not found in combination. We had such a leader in *the* Doctor. His intellect *and* spiritual understanding are . . . what merits the use of the definite article. Of course, it was the man who preceded the meeting . . . and the meeting took its shape and character from him. But it was the Lord who prepared him for this great part of his life's work.[18]

The Doctor was immensely self-disciplined and well-prepared when it came to his own preaching. But, as Hywel Jones observes:

In the Fellowship he was at his most unpredictable and versatile. In the discussions he was at times humorous, even on occasion outrageously so; sarcastic, but never savage; uncomfortably challenging; at times elusive and deliberately vague, at other times dogmatic and immovable at one point, while being quite open—infuriatingly so to some—on another matter. He did us the honour of expecting us to understand that however he spoke, it was in order to make us think.[19]

As we shall see later, this is exactly how the Doctor treated his own grandchildren, as we sat around the family table at Balsham. As with the Fraternal, he never knew what we would bring up for discussion, but his mind was quick enough, and his spiritual discernment so gifted, that he would be able to get right to the heart of the matter in a way that enabled us to see how he had arrived at his conclusion. In fact, outside the pulpit, he never taught by telling people what to think or how to respond, but by leading them through questions, so that in the end they taught themselves.

This was, once again, the diagnostic method. As Hywel Jones correctly points out, this was, 'in its basic features, both scientific and spiritual. The uniqueness of his methodology lay in the combination of these factors.'[20]

His scientific training was therefore at the heart of his

problem-solving, even though he was always to point to a spiritual solution. First of all, as a good scientist always does, one must find out as much as one can about the issue—one must never leap in with an opinion not based on the facts. 'How often,' Jones recalls, 'we felt reproved at the slender and partial basis on which we made our judgements!'[21]

(This is also what made him such a good parent and grandparent. He would never rush to conclusions, and always wanted to find out what had *really* happened first. The nature and character of the child was also important—while A would do something, B would not. This made him supremely fair—how often are family resentments built up when a child or grandchild feels unfairly treated. It was of course one of the reasons why his family loved him so much.)

Secondly, there was the importance of the 'indirect method'. This meant that the Doctor 'repeatedly reminded' the assembled ministers 'of the need to be general in one's approach to a subject before concentrating more narrowly upon it'.[22] The context of something was vital. This applied to preaching too. Ministers, as Hywel Jones reminds us, all too easily make a biblical text into a hobby horse by ignoring the context in which the biblical passage appears.

After the events of 1966 (see Chapter 8), the meetings obviously could not go on having members from mixed denominations. To those who had to leave, this was a tremendous loss. But logically it was a step that had to happen, otherwise the split would have dominated the discussions and made the work of the Fellowship impossible.

But, as Hywel Jones has pointed out, the Doctor was very aware of the dangers of secession. 'We were,' he writes, 'often required by the Doctor to do two things.

The first was to look at the situation to see if there was any material change in it.'[23] Secondly, were those who had seceded getting into proper fellowship with one another?

> Secession was the road to unity, the Doctor taught us, and not the path to isolationism and exclusivism. We saw that we could not go back without denying principles of truth which could not be more closely bound up with the Gospel, but I wonder whether we saw as clearly that we must go on. The Doctor impressed on us that we had been brought out in order to be brought in. Unless we went on to show the glory of the Gospel in the churches, how could we expect any to join us?[24]

In the family we were well aware of the extent to which he helped those who had followed him out in 1966. One of our abiding images of him is on the telephone in the living room of his home in Ealing. Ministers would ring up regularly and speak to him for what seemed to his grandchildren, eager to see their 'Dacu', hours on end! As always, he was the fount of wisdom for the poor, perplexed pastor on the other end of the phone line. Much of what he said was in the form of a question, and the result usually was that after much discussion—during which the enquirer often did most of the talking—the caller in question had solved his own problem! It had of course been the careful set of questions put to him by the Doctor that had led to the result—Martyn Lloyd-Jones was the brilliant diagnostician to the end. Once again, in his role as pastor's pastor, the Lord had prepared him through his training at Bart's.

Finally, as Hywel Jones has said, the close relationship the Doctor had with the ministers existed not just in the Fraternal and on the telephone, but

> better still in our homes. He listened to us and soon one knew one was talking to a valued, trusted and beloved friend.

Now that is over—for a little while. When we meet again we will not need to ask him any questions. We will be before the Lord; the ultimate answer to every problem will be provided and we shall know as we are known but we shall together share in 'wonder, love and praise' for ever.[25]

The Puritan Conference

This was another of the regular meetings at Westminster Chapel, becoming known after 1966 as 'the Westminster Conference'.

Although the Doctor always described himself as 'an eighteenth-century man'—a follower of Daniel Rowlands, Jonathan Edwards and the like—there is no doubt that he played a key role in bringing back biblical, Reformed thinking into evangelical life. As J. I. Packer has pointed out in his brilliant essay of the same name, the Doctor was 'A Kind of Puritan'.

The interest the Doctor created after the war in Puritan life and thought has thankfully continued after his death. Ironically, some of Puritanism's most powerful protagonists in the 1990s are Anglicans, men like J. I. Packer, and Alister McGrath who teaches at Wycliffe Hall at Oxford but whose book *Roots That Refresh* makes a strong case for the need of Evangelicalism at the end of the twentieth century to get back to the biblical roots that the Puritans discovered in their own day.

For as the Doctor discovered, the Puritans in turn always lead one back to the Scriptures, and to a vibrant, living, life-changing relationship with the living God. As D. A. Carson, another great enthusiast for Puritan thought has put it, the Puritans believed in 'the spirituality of the word'. It is the Bible that tells us what we need to know, and for the Puritans biblical spirituality was at the very heart of what Puritanism was all about.

Furthermore, as the Doctor never tired of pointing out, the Puritans had the biblical balance right—something that today we forget at our severe peril. They had both head and heart doctrine with what they called 'experimental' Christianity. One believed the proper doctrines, but one lived them too. As Christopher Hill points out in his essay on the importance of the Sabbath to the Puritan view of the world, their spirituality had the most profound effect on every single aspect of their lives. Even though not a Christian himself, Hill understood fully that it was spirituality and their Christian worldview that controlled Puritan economic thought and not the other way round.

As is obvious, the Puritan mix of doctrine and life is exactly the mix of 'logic on fire' that made the Doctor the unique man he was. So it is supremely fitting that it should have been Martyn Lloyd-Jones who played such a key role in restoring Puritan perspectives to Christian faith.

We have already seen that as far back as the 1930s Dr Lloyd-Jones would be found sitting on a beach, fully clothed and reading Reformed theology! But while he himself was deeply influenced by the Puritans, it was not until after the war that the movement back to a more biblical theology began. In this his daughter Elizabeth, then a student at Oxford, played a part, because it was the profound impact of the Puritans on some of her friends, and one in particular, that provided the impetus.

This was J. I. Packer, now one of the most eminent Evangelicals of our day. At the time, he was a rather bookish student at Oxford. He had real problems with the teaching that made Christians feel all the time that they had to 'surrender' to God, and all should be well. In fact, life being what it is, this is seldom the case. But in

God's providence, an elderly clergyman who was going blind gave a set of his old theological volumes to the library of the Oxford Inter Collegiate Christian Union (OICCU), of which Jim Packer and Elizabeth Lloyd-Jones were a part. Among the books donated was an uncut set of the writings of John Owen, the great seventeenth-century Puritan.

One of the treatises that Owen had written was on 'indwelling sin'—the Puritans, being biblical realists, knew that sin was an ongoing problem throughout life, and not something that one can just 'surrender' and forget about, as was then being taught. As Packer once told me, this was a turning point in his life. He had become a 'very isolated person' in Christian circles, because he knew that the instant sanctification teaching going around simply was not true, either to life or to his own Christian experience. But reading John Owen showed him that it was his experience that was in fact biblical. This revolutionised his life and greatly enhanced his own spiritual life and awareness.

Some other students had had similar experiences, so they went to the Doctor to discuss them. The Doctor had in fact been showing the faults in the same pastorally unhelpful teaching in his series at Westminster Chapel on 1 John (now published in several volumes as *Life in Christ*)—one of the series that Packer was many years later to describe as the Doctor on a 'plateau of supreme excellence'.

As Packer recalls, his own first meeting with the Doctor—along with another friend of Elizabeth's, the late Raymond Johnston—was in the vestry at Westminster Chapel. Packer and Johnston had come 'both still students . . . to float before his very eyes our vision of an annual Puritan Studies conference, and to seek his help in making it a reality. I was struck at the time by the

air of suppressed excitement with which he welcomed the
idea, as well as by his extreme forthcomingness: not only
would he host us at Westminster Chapel, but he would be
permanent chairman.'

Indeed he was to be Chairman for the next twenty-nine
years. Many years later, when the conference had grown
from twenty people to over 200, he told Packer that the
interest the two young men had shown 'in publicizing
Puritan standards of faith and devotion' was 'one of a
series of signs that God was starting to revive His work in
Britain, and therefore he had given it all the backing he
could'.[26] As Packer continues, 'At no stage did his interest
flag, and the historical acumen which his opinions and
conference contributions reflected was always of very high
order.'

Furthermore, as Packer points out, the Doctor truly
'had a flair for bringing history to life at a popular
level' and this is vital. Although he had loved history
since childhood, the Doctor did not regard his interest
in the Puritans as primarily historical, but in fact as being
profoundly practical. For since what the Puritans taught
was true, it was thus of supreme relevance to us today in
the twentieth century. The Puritans had made the truths
of Scripture come alive in their own generation, and his
vision was to do the same for his own. Many of his
sermons are steeped in Puritan theology—biblical truth
in twentieth-century language. (Although he himself used
the Authorised/King James Version all his life, his preaching was always contemporary in language. It was not the
language of the Puritans which mattered, but the life-
changing and life-enhancing message.)

He loved the Puritan conferences. Many of his talks—
he usually delivered the final paper—are in print today,
notably in *The Puritans and Their Successors*. (Packer's
talks are also in print, in *Among God's Giants*—known as

The Quest for Godliness in the USA.) The Doctor put an enormous amount of work into his addresses, and they were always backed up by considerable historical research. I remember going with him on several occasions to a library for ministers in London, where he would borrow a great number of books as part of his reading matter.

Another way in which the Doctor supported the revival of Puritan thought was through the foundation of the Banner of Truth, a publishing house designed partly to reprint many of the great Puritan classics, but also to disseminate Reformed thinking generally. With characteristic generosity, he gave this new publishing venture many of his own books—the great series on Romans and Ephesians being among them. (Iain Murray, his biographer, and a founder of the Banner of Truth Trust, was his assistant at Westminster Chapel for several years.) Many of those at the Puritan conferences had been converted to the Reformed cause through Banner of Truth publications. As R. T. France, now Principal of Wycliffe Hall in Oxford but then a student, once told me: in those days 'we were all Banner men'.

In conclusion, it is worth emphasising that the Doctor was always a Bible man first and last. He believed what he did because the Bible said so. This was why he so loved the Puritans—because they both taught and lived out what the Bible taught. But it was that way round. He did not start with the Puritans, and then read Scripture— never! He was indeed 'a kind of Puritan', but he was a 'Bible Puritan'. However much we may admire people— and with the Puritans it is right that we should—we must always remember, as the Doctor did, that we are to be followers of God's word rather than man's. As the Puritans would have believed, echoing the great Reformers who preceded them, *Sola Scriptura* and *Soli Deo Gloria*—Scripture alone and to God alone be the glory.

It would be ironic if in our reverence of the Puritans, we elevate them to biblical status, and therefore overturn all the principles on which they continued the Reformation. The Doctor did not make that mistake, and nor should we.

6

The International Fellowship of Evangelical Students

The beginnings

For many people, the lasting legacy of Martyn Lloyd-Jones was his preaching ministry, both at Westminster Chapel and thereafter through the printed versions of his sermons. Certainly, so far as those who have heard his name, this is true. But there are in the world today hundreds of thousands of evangelical students who have never heard his name so much as mentioned, but whose lives have been profoundly changed by the work which he helped to begin, and whose character he shaped.

The IFES—the International Fellowship of Evangelical Students—is one of the most significant Christian organisations in the world today. It is in fact unique, and one of the reasons for this is that during its formative years, Martyn Lloyd-Jones was in a position of key leadership and influence.

One of the things that makes IFES special is its leadership, which is wholly indigenous. The head office staff is minute, because the leaders of the movement are 'in the field' and are natives of the country in which they live, or at least from the same continent when it comes to senior posts. The organisation is federal, in that it consists not of a tight group at the top, composed mainly of Christians from the West, but rather of a coming together of

95

independent *local* organisations, united in fellowship together with a common purpose: the evangelism of the student world.

It is also truly worldwide. In 1985, four years after the Doctor's death, nearly 300,000 students were linked in some way to a movement affiliated to the IFES. With the fall of Communism in many countries, this is now larger still. Indeed if one takes 'underground' student groups into account as well, there is hardly a country in the world today in which an IFES-affiliated group does not exist.

Lastly, while only evangelical Christians may hold leadership positions, the membership is completely inter-denominational. It represents *all* Evangelicals, not just a section of them. For an organisation as international as IFES, this is in itself a remarkable achievement. This in turn means that it represents all different cultures and worship styles, with no one model being normative. It has Lutherans and Pentecostals, Anglicans and Baptists alike, not to mention churches formed in Third World countries which are indigenous in leadership but thoroughly united with other Evangelicals in theology.

The great movement that is now IFES began with a small conference in 1939, in Cambridge. This was symbolic, in that the origins of evangelical work among students had begun in the nineteenth century with what is now called the Cambridge Inter-Collegiate Christian Union—the CICCU. The conference was held in the shadow of a rapidly-approaching world war; one that would be more terrible than anything before. Among the 800 in attendance were students from both Britain and Germany; nations that would be fighting each other within months. All kinds of churches were represented there, with delegates coming from both State churches and Free Churches alike. With the world around them at loggerheads, the delegates were united.

Dr Lloyd-Jones was present in his capacity as President of the Inter-Varsity Fellowship—the British movement. Fittingly, in view of the international situation, the Doctor's text was especially relevant. He preached on 'The One Essential'; on the need to have Jesus Christ both as our Saviour and our Lord.

As Chua Wee-Hian—General Secretary of IFES from 1971 to 1991—has put it, the fact that the Doctor was Welsh made a huge difference. Many organisations were very Western dominated, meaning domination by either English people or Americans. The Doctor felt acutely the Welsh oppression by the English in what for him was living memory. (My great-grandmother Margaret Phillips, whom I remember well from childhood, had to wear what is called 'the Welsh Knot'—a wooden placard around the neck for those caught speaking Welsh in school. Welsh was not in fact given equal status in the Law Courts until the 1960s. Such things understandably deeply rankled with the Welsh, especially those from predominantly Welsh-speaking backgrounds like the Doctor.)

Consequently, he identified strongly with the Christians from colonial countries. Racism was entirely alien to him. He did not make the mistake, as some well-meaning First World people have done, of condescending to folk from different cultures or with other skin colours—something that is in itself a form of racism, however kindly intended. No, to him all people were equal in the sight of God, and all Christians, regardless of race, were his brothers and sisters in Christ.

As we have seen, the Doctor was also very firm on doctrinal issues. In this he had an ally in the great Norwegian Christian leader, O. Hallesby. A strong emphasis on doctrine, and on the supremacy of Scripture, was to be a hallmark of the work of the IFES throughout its history.

When the expected war finally broke out in 1939, plans that had been made at the Cambridge conference obviously had to be shelved. It was in a very different world that delegates met again in April 1946. Several of the delegates present only seven years earlier were now dead. Europe was in tatters, with even the countries that had won the war in a state of ruin and great poverty.

But despite the horrors of a world war, and of the Holocaust, the vision of reaching the student world for Christ lived on. The Doctor was one of the three delegates from Britain at this conference. Everyone was unanimous that a new, thoroughly international body should be formed—the IFES. Thus was a great movement born out of the ashes of war and the folly of a godless humanity.

The foundation of IFES

Chua Wee-Hian has called the Doctor 'one of the founding fathers of IFES'. The first General Secretary, Stacey Woods, who led the movement for its first twenty-five years—as well as leading the American IVCF for a while—has written of the Doctor's contribution:

> No history of the IFES would be complete without some account of its first Chairman, Dr. Martyn Lloyd-Jones. . . . He did more to lay a solid biblical foundation . . . than anyone else . . . his influence and leadership in the growing young international movement was great. From his busy life, not only was he always available as an occasional speaker to students, but always for counsel to the general secretary. He freely gave several days each year to the executive committee and longer periods to the general committee which student delegates attended every three to four years.[27]

As Chua Wee-Hian has added, the Doctor was also very sensitive to those whose first language was not English, the language used at committee meetings. He knew that they needed extra time to formulate their thoughts and to understand what was going on. Once again, the Doctor's Welshness was a great influence here. Although he normally preached in English, his language at home, with his wife and daughters, continued to be Welsh until his death. (With his grandchildren he spoke English, as neither daughter married a Welsh speaker.)

Dr Lloyd-Jones was very much 'in at the foundation'. As Chua Wee-Hian has written in *With Evangelical Students*, in the 'debates and discussions that took place, it was the good Doctor who presented proposals, clause by clause' for the new constitution. The minutes of the 1946 conference recorded that the 'Committee was greatly indebted to the able, patient and very clear manner in which Dr. Lloyd-Jones presented the amendments',[28] something far from easy at an international meeting.

The IFES did not formally exist and this was to be ratified by an official meeting that took place in the USA, at Harvard, in August 1947. In 1946 the Doctor had been proposed as the Vice-Chairman of the new body. But as the original Chairman could not be present, it was in fact Dr Lloyd-Jones who presided over the international assembly. This was providential, as his influence as Chairman was thus all the greater. He was to serve as the founder Chairman of IFES from 1947 to 1959, as President from 1959 to 1967, and then as a Vice-President for the rest of his life.

Chua Wee-Hian has well described this foundational assembly:

At Harvard the participants affirmed the importance of being both a *biblical* and *genuinely international* movement [my

italics]. All member movement of the IFES had to be unreservedly committed to the supreme authority of the holy
Scriptures. Sound doctrine, combined with Spirit-generated
warmth, must characterise each national affiliate. But in
addition, conscious as [the Doctor] was of the possible
domination of powerful countries over the weaker ones, the
Doctor guided the General Committee to accept the need for
an 'open' Fellowship. Each movement must be encouraged to
develop its own style of leadership, suited to its cultural
ethos; no group should impose on another its pattern of
work. So the basic quality of indigineity [leadership by
people from that country] was affirmed at the very outset
of this organisation.[29]

When one reads the accounts of missionary churches in
the Third World, this principle of local leadership is all
the more remarkable, in that many a missionary organisation did not want local Christians to have control over
the new churches that were being formed, and such disputes often went on well into the 1960s, sometimes after
that particular country had received independence from
the colonial power in question. Often there was much
bitterness that did the gospel no good, as some of the
local churches became a mix of Christian practice and
pagan superstition, as well as fostering the utterly false
view that Christianity is a 'white man's religion', rather
than being God's revealed truth to the whole of mankind.
Thanks to the Doctor, the IFES avoided these disputes
from the very beginning, and in fact IFES is often
strongest in countries outside the West. (The biggest
Christian Union group on any campus is in Singapore,
and the Nigerian IFES movement is one of the largest.)

Stacey Woods has described the Doctor at work. He
had, Woods wrote,

great skill as a chairman, patient so long as the speaker dealt
with the matter in hand, but insistent that time was not

wasted with irrelevant gabble. He loved keen debate, liked to be challenged, but woe betide the opponent who entered into the lists of debate with him unprepared but full of self-confidence. . . . In spite of that keen, incisive mind, our chairman was a leader in committee, not director or dictator.[30]

We can see in more detail from the Harvard conference the principles to which Chua Wee-Hian has referred. The Doctor was asked to help draw up the IFES basis of faith and action. The aims of IFES were to be clear from the start.

First, they were to encourage 'Christian fellowship and helpful association' between existing Christian groups, referred to as National Evangelical Unions (NEUs). Secondly, there was 'a great missionary evangelistic work to be done in the many countries where there [were] as yet no NEUs, and in other countries where NEUs [were] weak'[31] and needed help.

But then came the revolutionary concept for the church of those days: 'The task of IFES is to initiate and to help national evangelical unions *that are to be autonomous* [my italics] and, once they are established, withdraw from any direct action except at the request of the said national committee when aid or co-operation in some new activity were asked.'[32]

The Doctor and the uniqueness of IFES

This has been a guiding principle of IFES ever since. It accounts for the movement's growth, in that unlike many other organisations, it cannot be accused of being a tool of powerful Western countries. While the General Secretary of IFES is always an influential figure, there is no question of rule from headquarters. Nor is there any 'power of the purse strings', with notional local leadership but real power being held by the paymaster in the West. Such concepts are alien to the IFES, frustrating though this has been at times for members from the wealthier and more powerful nations!

The two other unique features of the IFES go together—its interdenominational approach and the fact that it is firmly rooted in Scripture. It is because it is so strongly biblically based that it can be interdenominational, since its members concentrate far more on what they have in common with each other than on the issues over which they differ. This again was greatly influenced by Dr Lloyd-Jones.

In the chapter on 1966 and the nature of the church, we will see in more detail the Doctor's view on matters denominational, and on where he felt the boundaries should be drawn. In 1966 the Doctor urged Evangelicals to withdraw from doctrinally 'mixed' denominations which contained Evangelicals and Liberals alike. However, he continued both to hold office in the IFES, and speak at their conferences, for the rest of his life. This was despite the fact that individuals in the IFES were in all kinds of denominations, both purely evangelical and thoroughly 'mixed' alike. (Many of the members from Scandinavian countries were members of their Lutheran State churches.) But in fact there was no contradiction.

This was because the member *movements* themselves had to be evangelically pure. It was also because the IFES recognised only evangelical belief as a criterion for membership, rather than denominational affiliation. In fact its official view on this was quite clear. Its foundational document reads: 'The church of Christ consists of all those who in all ages have been or are in vital relationship with our Lord Jesus Christ as a result of the "new birth".'[33] Church membership was in only two recognised categories—the fellowship worldwide of all believers, and the local church. Christ was present in both.

In other words, what mattered was gospel unity, based on the common experience of salvation in Christ, and of Christ's lordship. Also vital was the doctrine of Scripture, which IFES took to be of supreme importance. It was what the Bible said that mattered rather than any man-made tradition.

The issue of evangelical purity came up very early in the history of the movement, when a large Finnish Lutheran organisation wished to join. The student body was a member of the World Student Christian Federation, a theologically liberal body, which therefore precluded membership of IFES. As a former IFES General Secretary has written, the situation was not easy. The proponent of entry was himself an Evangelical, and 'like all new international bodies, IFES could do with new members'![34] But IFES decided that it had to stick to its foundational evangelical principles and refuse the Finnish body entry. 'And yet the Doctor did not close the door to the Finnish Evangelicals. He urged them to rethink their position, and indeed suggested publicly that they should continue to have personal and informal links with IFES.'[35]

Significantly, the theologically mixed body has declined since then, whereas the completely evangelical Finnish Lutheran Student Mission, which joined IFES in 1964, has continued to grow. But the Doctor's own attitude, and his Christian love for the Finns, is also important. Rather than denounce them, he kept the door open, with the very positive results that flowed from it.

The Doctor on the IFES Executive

In fact the Doctor was to listen with sympathy to students from even more divergent backgrounds who were joining

IFES. Chua Wee-Hian has described in *With Evangelical Students* some of the conversations he had with the Doctor during his own twenty years as IFES General Secretary. It is truly revealing.

The issue had arisen in some countries of students from Catholic backgrounds assuming the leadership of some of the campus Christian fellowships. Chua writes:

> The Doctor rejoiced to hear of large numbers of these students turning to Christ and experiencing new birth and new life. Many of these students would have no qualms in signing an evangelical basis of faith. This meant that they could become active members and even leaders in our local groups. But what of their links with a church that still subscribes to certain tenets that are contrary to Scripture? If they did not know the difference between these and the fundamentals of the evangelical faith, should they not be disqualified from holding office?[36]

The Doctor was naturally interested in what the IFES Executive Committee thought of all this. The answer was that it was summoning its members to an even greater evangelical awareness, and in 'positively teaching the central truths of revealed faith we had to expose erroneous doctrines'.

The Doctor was 'supportive of this approach. But even before [Chua Wee-Hian] could amplify the pastoral dimension of the problem, his sharp mind had anticipated this.'

'You do know,' said the Doctor, 'that if Catholic students were to repudiate the doctrines of their church, that could also be interpreted as a rejection of their families.'[37]

Some instances of this, in Catholic countries, came to Chua Wee-Hian. So the 'Doctor further advised' IFES 'to make sure that these Catholic students felt accepted as persons. They must be encouraged to search the

Scriptures. As they grow, then they must discern truth from error.'[38]

In other words, as opposed to simply booting them out, they were to be accepted as brothers and sisters in Christ, and in their own time, through getting to grips with God's word, follow logically what the Bible was saying to them. At no stage was there to be any kind of fudge, abandoning clear evangelical truth, and bending the doctrinal basis in order to let people in. But at the same time there was also great pastoral sensitivity, and a profound willingness to accept people as they were.

The evening prior to the Executive Committee, the Doctor would insist that all the members get together *not* to discuss business, but to pray, and also to talk over important theological issues. This was so that they could then go on to discuss things the next day in the right context, having first set the proper spiritual tenor for the work in hand. Stacey Woods has written: 'Decisions and questions on the following day seemed clearer, answers more obvious, as a result of the stimulus and enlightened conversation of the previous evening.'[39]

Another special feature of his chairmanship is that he was very wary of long-term planning, and of trying to project what things would be like ten years ahead. This especially applied if those wanting long-term plans came from the prosperous Western nations. He felt that if the IFES was open to the call of the Holy Spirit and remained true to Scripture, they might find themselves having to change plans because the Lord had decided to lead them in a direction which they had not foreseen. What if something extraordinary happened, and they were tied into a programme of action from which they could not shift? (This was the same principle that he applied for himself at Westminster Chapel—he was always reluctant to announce what he would preach on the next Sunday, let alone for weeks or months ahead.)

While this might seem strange to some, events at the end of the 1980s bear this out strongly. Who would, even at the beginning of 1989, have predicted that the Iron Curtain would fall; that countries like Hungary and Czechoslovakia would be democracies, and that within a very short time, even the Soviet Union itself would disintegrate and Communism fall? But, to the Doctor, with his very strong sense of God's sovereignty, nothing was surprising. Although he did not live to see the events just described, he knew that God *could* do anything, and that while one should always make due provision for the future, such plans should never be so rigid that one could not be open to a fresh leading of the Spirit, and to new opportunities that the Lord might send.

In 1959 the Doctor stepped down as Chairman to become President. At that year's General Committee he addressed them on biblical authority; talks that were later to be published as a book with the same name, still in print over thirty years later.

The Executive Committee, 'conscious of its privilege of association with Dr. Lloyd-Jones during the last twelve years' and of the 'leadership, counsel and inspiration he had given to IFES', unanimously passed a resolution which stated that it wished to 'express its thanks and appreciation to him and to his wife for the generous giving of themselves to this work', and to him personally for 'his leadership, not only in the committee as chairman but more particularly for his spiritual leadership and direction in the work as a whole'.[40]

Furthermore, not only was he to be the President, but as his talks were greatly valued, he was asked by the Executive to 'be with us and address us at each general committee meeting [every four years] and whenever possible to be present at future meetings of the executive committee. We would also assure him,' the Committee continued, 'that we feel the need of his continued leadership and counsel in the work, and therefore in no sense do we regard him as having retired from IFES.'[41]

Nor in fact did he ever do this. He remained either President or Vice-President until his death, continuing to come to meetings and to advise the General Secretary on all matters of importance.

One of the most notable occasions that he did this was the General Committee of 1971, held in the beautiful Austrian castle, Schloss Mittersill, up in the mountains. One of the special things about the meeting was that so many of the Doctor's old friends were there. These men were the pioneers, who had built up this now great organisation from scratch and changed the lives of thousands of students over those twenty-five years. This sense of camaraderie, of long-standing fellowship in the Lord's work, was special to the Doctor as it was to all of us. Some of the people involved were real characters, and as we have seen, the Doctor always loved such folk, ever since the days of the spitting village blacksmith in Newcastle Emlyn! Stacey Woods, the retiring General Secretary, was certainly a character—the Christian student world is full of 'Stacey stories' of this larger-than-life man.

Pioneers are not always the easiest of people to work with, and Stacey Woods fell into that category. But the Doctor was always able to use the immense talents that Woods also possessed to steer the work in the right direction. Woods always loved a drama. I remember one Mittersill conference I attended where there were some delegates from Communist countries present. Had their presence been known back home, they would have been in real trouble. A student from a Third World country was also at the conference, and it emerged that he had been suborned by the Secret Police of one Communist regime to be a spy. He was caught going down to the village to file reports on some of the delegates. Stacey Woods, as well as being deeply concerned, also revelled in all the drama of a spy in our midst! One got the impression that he dined out on it for years. Yet without the sheer energy and exuberance of Stacey Woods, combined with the spiritual—and sometimes calming—influence of Dr Lloyd-Jones, the work of IFES could never have been what it has turned out to be.

Another old faithful was John Bolten, who also served for many years on the Executive Committee. He was now a retired and immensely successful businessman in the USA, who gave away much of his wealth for the Lord's work. But he had been born a German and, as a young man, had personally known Hitler. (He fascinated me by giving me Hitler's handshake, which was surprising by being so limpid.) In God's providence, he had come to see what Nazism was really like and had fled the country. He too had collaborated with the Doctor for many years in the work of IFES, and was here to pay his tributes.

This year—1971—was the Silver Jubilee of the IFES, and thus a very special occasion. Although not a delegate myself, I was present at the conference, and got to know students from all over the world, some of them from countries where preaching an evangelical gospel was very hard. Chua Wee-Hian, who took over as General Secretary at the meeting, has given a wonderful description of the event; one that not only tells us of the important spiritual truths that the Doctor conveyed to the assembled delegates and staff, but also a very human picture of him—one that shows why the Doctor was not only highly respected but deeply loved.

Just before the General Committee there was a special staff consultation. Each morning Dr. Lloyd-Jones spoke to us on what it meant to be an Evangelical Christian. He warned us against the pitfall of 'Evangelical respectability'. Evangelical scholarship had already made its mark in the theological world. Evangelical leadership was evidently penetrating ecclesiastical structures in several countries. Like the children of Israel, it was possible for us to forget God in the midst of our apparent successes. He exhorted us to be valiant for truth; we must never allow our doctrines to be diluted by persuasive philosophies. We were to study God's Word with diligence and to proclaim it with boldness, clarity and urgency [according to 2 Timothy 4:2].[42]

The student delegates at the Committee heard the Doctor expound 1 Samuel 4. He spoke to them about the 'absence of God'. It was possible for Christians to be so preoccupied with themselves and their activities—even Christian ones—that they left God out of their reckoning. 'That message was used by God's Spirit,' Chua Wee-Hian recalls, 'to convict many of us of sin and insensitivity to [God's] glory. It resulted in confession and repentance, and a new sense of joy.'[43]

We have seen how the Doctor's preaching, both in Aberavon and at Westminster Chapel, gave its hearers a powerful sense of the glory of God—it was one of the great hallmarks of his ministry. All this was preached not in a church, but in a very modern auditorium, so it was the preaching that gave the sense of God, and not the surroundings—though the beautiful mountain scenery did help remind one of God's handiwork.

Chua Wee-Hian continues with memories that mean a lot to the Doctor's grandchildren. We knew 'Dacu' to be someone of immense warmth, and with a powerful, if not actually impish sense of humour. As we have seen, the Doctor never made jokes in the pulpit, and this gave him a somewhat austere reputation. But he could relax among friends, and at the IFES Silver Jubilee General Committee he was exactly that.

Chua writes that one evening,

> the Doctor paid tribute to the retiring General Secretary, Stacey Woods. The entire assembly roared with uncontroll- able laughter as Dr Lloyd-Jones proceeded to relate anecdotes about the founding fathers of the Fellowship. One British leader had been so self-effacing that he would lock himself in a toilet when a group photograph was being taken. On another occasion a well-known Hungarian professor was reeling like a drunken sailor when he accidentally bumped into the Doctor. The latter was at first perplexed with the behaviour of his colleague, whom he knew to be a teetotaller! His analytical mind then recalled that a few delegates had complained about upset stomachs caused by the conference food. The abilities of the Doctor as a master story teller endeared him to all.[44]

That conference shows the Doctor at his best in many ways. It shows his prophetic genius, open to what God was *really* saying to his people rather than what they were wanting to hear. Popularity is dangerous! We can lose our biblical direction and be led astray. As always, he pointed them back to the Scripture, and gave that profound sense of the glory of God that we have observed. He could also be pastoral. Some of the founding fathers had personal griefs in their lives, and no one was better equipped to help them through than Dr Lloyd-Jones. But he was also a warm, lovable human being; a friend as well as leader, not too aloof to tell jokes and to enter into the fun of the occasion.

The Doctor always kept his love of IFES. His family shared this with him. His son-in-law, Fred Catherwood, served on many IFES committees over many years, sev- eral of them also on the Executive Committee, as IFES Treasurer, retiring in 1993. All three Catherwood grand- children attended IFES conferences at the castle in Mit- tersill. (I went to over ten, which I am told is not far off the record!) In my case, I became active in giving support to Christian groups in some Central European countries then under Communist rule. I made many friends for life, and my experiences there considerably changed my outlook, helping me, I am sure, to grow spiritually. It changed me in other ways too. I developed an academic interest in the lands of the old Habsburg Empire; one that I have maintained through all the tragic events that happened in some of them in the 1990s. My family sometimes used to worry when I went off behind the Iron Curtain to visit Christians there, but my grandfather, with his strong sense of God's protection over his people, knew that I was in the safest possible hands.

That perspective is, of course, a vital one, and shows the environment the Doctor had created in IFES. There was, as we have seen, no nonsense about Western Christians having it all. Far from it! At many of those conferences, it was we who learned from our friends in the Third World and in the 'suffering church', of countries where the gospel could not be freely preached, but where the church was often growing in spite of persecution. Being in a Bible study with people like that made Western Christians—including those of us from famous groups like the Oxford Inter-Collegiate Christian Union—feel very small.

But fellowship at such conferences was also great fun. Like the Doctor himself, we formed friendships from literally all over the world, including with people whose ability to communicate in English was rather limited, but whose godliness radiated from them. One of the many humbling things about such conferences was that we realised how easy we English speakers had it. We listened to folk stumbling over English phrases, then realised when we tried to speak back to them in our even more limited Serbo-Croat or Arabic that their linguistic skills were far superior to our own! Any lurking Anglo-Saxon feelings of superiority were always cured by a fortnight at Mittersill. Many of us are still in touch with people we befriended over twenty years ago.

The work of IFES is in a sense a glorious foretaste of heaven, with people from every country and race, with all their different languages, histories, cultures and experiences, but united in the most important thing of all: the saving work of our common Lord Jesus Christ. This was, of course, the vision of the Doctor himself.

As we will see in the chapter on 1966, the Doctor had a magnificent vision of an evangelical church, in which every group maintained its own distinctives, and even had separate denominations, but nevertheless came together as Evangelicals united around the gospel. As we will also see, this great appeal failed, and drove a wedge among Evangelicals in Britain from which it is only now slowly recovering.

But in IFES, his glorious vision of a united evangelicalism came gloriously true. It really was the evangelical, Christ-centred, gospel-orientated organisation of his dreams. He came to believe that Evangelicals should withdraw from doctrinally 'mixed' denominations. But as we have seen, IFES recognised only the gathered church of all believers, and the local church. Denominations did not come into the picture. To join IFES one had to be evangelical, and that was what mattered. (He would have been pleased that the current IFES General Secretary, Lindsay Brown, is a Welshman! They became acquainted during Lindsay's student days, and Dr Lloyd-Jones came to Oxford to speak to the Christian Union, the OICCU, during Lindsay's presidency. In this way, although Lindsay became General Secretary ten years after the Doctor's death, my grandfather has known all the holders of the post so far.)

So by not confronting the divisive issue of denomination, but instead concentrating on the unifying work of Christ, his vision was not only fulfilled, but continues today, stronger than ever. The IFES represented all that the Doctor stood for and believed in throughout his years of ministry, and praise God that the vision lives on after him.

Martyn on the right. This photograph had to be retaken several times because he kept on pinching his baby brother!

Martyn in Harrow with his fiancée Bethan in front of him. Next to him is Ieuan Phillips, Bethan's brother; and on the right Vincent, Martyn's brother. Mrs Phillips, Bethan's mother is on the right of the front row.

Wedding day, 8th January 1927.

The young doctor at Barts.

*With John Bolten – who bought
Schloss Mittersill for IFES.*

Preaching at Westminster Chapel –
a characteristic pose.

*Sutton Hall, Balsham. The Catherwoods' home
where the Doctor spent much time.*

*With the Catherwood family.
Back row: Jonathan, Fred, Elizabeth, Christopher.
Front row: Bethan Catherwood, Bethan and Martyn Lloyd-Jones*

Ann Desmond.

The Desmond grandchildren.

The Doctor and his wife, taken in America in 1969.

7

Joy Unspeakable

1963

It was around midnight—if not the early hours of the morning. A rather frightened young student was making a call from a phone box. He had had an experience which had rather alarmed him. Only one person would know the answer, so despite the lateness of the hour—not to mention the fact that phone boxes were not the safest places to be around midnight—he made the call.

What had so perturbed him? Well, he had heard people making the most unusual sounds. In trying to heal someone of a broken limb, they had prayed out loud in what sounded like gibberish. The sheer outlandishness and eeriness of the experience and sounds were most unsettling, and the young man making the call knew that the one on the other end of the line would be able to explain to him what had been going on.

The alarmed young caller was me, and the recipient the Doctor himself. As we have seen, it was entirely reasonable for me to feel able to ring my grandfather from an Oxford call box after midnight! What I heard was what is described by some as the spiritual gift of tongues, and by others as a satanic counterfeit.

The scene changes. It was an unusually humid day in Tsimshatsui. The monsoon rains had been falling and to walk through them was like going through a sauna. I was about to go to the People's Republic of China and wanted some advice—I had been looking after the flat of an old Westminster Chapel missionary now on furlough. The person I was visiting was an Australian, who had lived in even more inhospitable climes than these.

Having inherited a good proportion of my grandmother Lloyd-Jones' fervid imagination, I imagined myself arrested as soon as I crossed the border. The Doctor himself was not far from death, and one of the things he had asked as I set off on this trip was, 'How long will he be?' It was, as we shall see later, as if he knew when he would die and wanted to make sure that he could see me before the moment came.

After assuring me that I was likely to be quite safe (the radio that I was supposed to take into China proved too heavy anyway), the Australian told me that it was now his turn to ask a question, and it was one that surprised me. Was it true that my grandfather had become a Pentecostal? I knew news travelled, but what had given him that idea?

Some years later, I was in a church in the USA not exactly known for its sympathy to things charismatic. A large and burly man came up to me. Was it true that the Doctor's book on the subject had been tampered with to make him sound pentecostal? Everyone knew, of course, that he was really nothing of the kind! Fortunately, I was rescued by a friend, who, while himself a firm cessationist on the subject of spiritual gifts, was able to say that nothing of the sort had happened. (This old chestnut went the rounds in some circles, despite the fact that the book relayed sermons that had been heard by over 2,500 people each Sunday in Westminster Chapel! It was finally scotched when the tapes of the sermons made clear that nothing had been altered.)

So here were two very different views of what the Doctor taught on the Holy Spirit—one that he had become pentecostal and the other that he was an anti-charismatic who had been hijacked. Obviously both views cannot be right!

So what did he tell me that late night, as the pennies mounted up in the phone box near the memorial to Cranmer and Ridley?

Well, the answer is to be found in those sermons, now published as *Joy Unspeakable* and *Prove All Things* (the latter known by the slightly more appropriate title in the USA of *The Sovereign Spirit*).

What has always astonished his family is that there was ever any misunderstanding at all. What he taught was there, plain as a pikestaff. Yes, he believed in the baptism of the Spirit as an experience separate from conversion, although sometimes quite close to it. Yes, he also believed that all Christians received the Holy Spirit on conversion. What he calls baptism with the Holy Spirit was something different. Yes, he did believe in the continuation of spiritual gifts. But, no, he did not believe that they could be claimed, on demand as it were, nor did he believe that the gift of tongues was the necessary evidence of baptism with the Spirit. As for whether something was genuine, we have seen that he believed all phenomena must be tested. So whether the tongues I heard were genuine or not he could not say, but yes, the gift still existed in principle.

But of course, that was far too simple for most people, and that is where the problem came in. Some of course knew his real views and felt that they should never have gone into print. He, though, had clearly intended them to appear, since the transcripts have his handwriting all over them, preparing them for publication. The fact of publication was made far worse, in their eyes, because the Editor of the book was the Doctor's own grandson. Treachery! (What occurred to none of them was that had they looked at the copyright page, they would have seen that it was in the name of Bethan Lloyd-Jones. She had what was probably the simplest attitude to all of it, which was to say, 'What is all the fuss? Why do people have to use all these words like "Reformed"? Why don't they just say "biblical"?' To which we all said, 'Amen!' Sadly, though, life was not as simple as she would have wished . . .)

He had of course made the very same points in his sermons on Romans and Ephesians, which were published in his own lifetime by the Banner of Truth. But he had not used any of the code words; the expressions designed to provoke the warring factions into battle. Instead of 'baptism' he had used another Pauline word, 'sealing'. Now to him—and, he felt, to Scripture—these were all the same thing. The British head of state is the Queen, the Sovereign, the Monarch, etc.—different titles but all denoting the same person. Likewise with 'baptism' and 'sealing'.

Thus to us, sitting around the family table in Balsham, near Cambridge, his views were clear. Not all of us agreed with him—his son-in-law, for example, took the Warfield view that charismatic gifts had ceased. But whether we agreed with him or not, what he was saying was based on his interpretation of Scripture.

Unfortunately, as Jim Packer has so ably pointed out in his book *Keep in Step with the Spirit*, some people are more influenced by tradition in what they believe than by what Scripture is actually saying, however inconvenient this might be. Calvin was a cessationist too, and to many that meant that if one was to be truly Reformed, one had to be a cessationist too. (Ironically, some of the people who held this view most strongly were Baptists. Now while to some of us there is no problem about being both Reformed and Baptist, Calvin was a firm paedobaptist! So while they were strongly denying that one could ever believe in continuing spiritual gifts and be Reformed, they were undermining their own case by their insistence that one could indeed be Reformed while denying the doctrine of infant baptism in which Calvin believed so strongly.)

So let us look at what the Doctor actually said in *Joy Unspeakable* and then go on to look at the way in which two people who knew him analysed the problem—his close collaborator over many years, Hywel Jones, and Bob Horn, now General Secretary of the UCCF, but at the time a minister who attended the regular Westminster Fellowship meetings.

The Doctor, as his son-in-law Fred Catherwood has put it, had come increasingly to feel that a certain aridity had entered the Christian church, including the Reformed wing of which he was a part.

So when, in his expositions of John's Gospel, he came to John 1:26 and 33, he felt that the time had come to return people to the kind of spiritual lives they ought to be leading. This was baptism with the Holy Spirit. To him this was 'no academic exercise'. Indeed, he made clear: 'It seems to me that this is the thing that we need above all else at the present time.'[45]

He then highlighted the real problem, which was in fact the entire problem with the people who reacted to him as they did. He said, 'Perhaps the greatest danger of all for Christian people is the danger of understanding the Scriptures in the light of their experiences, but we should examine our experiences in the light of the teaching of the Scripture.'[46] (This was, as we have seen earlier, what his wife thought too!)

The first danger was to go beyond Scripture and invent false teaching. The second was to put tradition on a level with Scripture.

However, some dangers were more subtle, and some

who fell into such traps were 'generally the most spiritually minded'. One such error was to become 'so interested
in the experimental [ie, experiential, a Puritan term] side
that they become indifferent to The Scripture. . . . Now
that is fanaticism, and it is a terrible danger which we
must always bear in mind. It arises from a divorce
between Scripture and experience, where we put experience above Scripture, claiming things that are not sanc-
tioned by Scripture, or are perhaps even prohibited by
it.'[47]

But, he went on, 'There is a second danger and it is
equally important that we should bear it in mind. The
second is the exact opposite of the first, as these things
generally go from one violent extreme to the other.' This,
by contrast, was 'that of being satisfied with something
very much less than what is offered in the Scripture, and
the danger of interpreting Scripture by our experiences
and reducing its teaching to the level of what we know
and experience.' He concluded, 'And I would say that this
second is the greater danger of the two at the present
time.'[48]

People were so terrified of the supernatural that they
were in danger of quenching the Holy Spirit. So alarmed
were they by fanaticism that they went 'right over to the
other side without facing what is offered in the New
Testament'. How many churches today would have to
have a letter written to them like 1 Corinthians? There
may have been excesses—Paul corrected them, but 'see
what he allows, what he expects'.[49]

Thus everything we believed 'must be tested by the
teaching of Scripture. We must not start with what we
think, what we like.'[50]

He then went on to look at what the Scriptures said. It
was of course true that as both Romans and 1 Corinthians
proved, 'no man can be a Christian at all apart from the

work of the Holy Spirit'.[51] So everyone had the Holy
Spirit. But he went on to show, from many illustrations
from Galatians, Ephesians and Acts, 'that you can be a
believer, that you can have the Holy Spirit dwelling in you,
and still not be baptised with the Holy Spirit'.[52] Antici-
pating criticism he went on to say to some imaginary
person—a rhetorical device of which he was very fond
in his preaching:

> Ah, you may say, now you have said that tongues are all right.
> I am sure that many are already thinking that. You wait a
> minute; I shall deal with the question of gifts when it comes
> at the right place. You do not start with that. That comes
> towards the end of this treatment. But that is how the devil
> gets us to bypass the Scriptures in the interests of our
> particular point of view, whichever of the two extremes it
> may chance to be.[53]

Then, using Acts 18 and Ephesians 1, he went on to show
from Scripture that his case was indeed a valid one, and
that 'you can be regenerate without being baptised with
the Holy Spirit. The Scriptures [that he had adduced]
show quite clearly that to say, as so many have said . . .
that every man at regeneration is of necessity baptised
with the Holy Spirit is simply to fly in the face of this
plain, explicit teaching of the Holy Scriptures.'[54]

However, that was by no means all. Later in the book,
and in the sequel, which was preached in the same sermon
series at Westminster Chapel, he also went on to show
that many tenets of classic pentecostal teaching were also
not in accord with Scripture, thereby putting himself, on
that issue, in the other camp. There was a great danger of
the counterfeit. As he made clear, one could not claim any
particular gift.

Furthermore, while 'there is no experience possible to
the Christian in this world higher than this experience of

the baptism with the Spirit', we as Christians 'should not seek primarily what he gives'.[55] For 'we should always be seeking the Lord Jesus Christ himself, to know him and know his love'.[56] Love was what mattered. Indeed as he put it:

> This is New Testament Christianity! New Testament Christianity is not just a formal, polite, correct and orthodox kind of faith and belief. No! What characterizes it is this element of love and passion, this pneumatic element, this life, this vigour, this abandon, this exuberance—and, as I say, it has ever characterized the life of the church in all periods of revival and of re-awakening. That is what we must seek—not experiences, not power, not gifts. If he chooses to give them to us, thank God for them, exercise them to his glory, but the only safe way of receiving gifts is that you love him and that you know him.[57]

Spiritual gifts certainly existed, therefore, but the idea that you could claim them, or that certain gifts were to be expected, was quite contrary to Scripture.

So quite how either side of the divide could claim him was a mystery to us. As his son-in-law has put it, 'That was totally to misunderstand his teaching—that both strands [Calvinist and charismatic] were absolutely essential parts of Christian belief, that the one called for the other, and that in each Christian life they had to be woven strongly together. Strength and warmth, warmth and strength.'[58]

Perhaps of course it was easy for the Doctor to believe things that few others combined. He did after all believe that preaching was logic on fire, and that meant in this context the logic of the Calvinist and the fire of the charismatic—though as he himself showed, Calvinists could have fire and those who believed in the continuation of charismatic gifts could possess logic! So his dual belief was quite consistent with the man, as well as flowing from Scripture.

This last point was the most crucial to him. As we have seen, he was a Bible Calvinist, not a system one. This made all the difference.

He once told the British Evangelical Council in an address later published as *What Is the Church?*:

> You and I are living in this evil hour in the history of the Christian church very largely because of what became of our grandfathers [this was 1968]. They held onto their orthodoxy, but many of them had lost the life. The only way you can safeguard yourself from a dead orthodoxy is to put life before even orthodoxy. All appeals for unity in the New Testament are based on life.[59]

This was not of course to say that orthodoxy is not important. Far from it! As we shall see in a forthcoming chapter, he was deeply concerned about orthodoxy. So much so that he was prepared to separate from others over what he regarded as a downplaying of essential biblical orthodoxy. But I think we all know what he meant: there was no point in being orthodox if one showed no signs of life.

As Hywel Jones once told me, the Doctor's main concern in the last years of his own life was for this; 'for life', spiritual life, life as lived in the New Testament. Hywel Jones was close to him, especially in his thinking. His essay on the Doctor, *The Pastor's Pastor*, is of great relevance to our whole understanding of what Martyn Lloyd-Jones thought about this whole, tragically divisive issue of the Holy Spirit. (As Jim Packer has pointed out, it has often become a litmus test for where someone is theologically—'What is your view on the charismatic issue?'—and how sad that is.)

In discussing the Westminster Fellowship, Hywel Jones writes of the Doctor's emphases: 'First and foremost was the importance of *spiritual life*.' So often we get bogged

down in man-centred religion. 'Though repudiating and
ridiculing the "God is dead" theology, Evangelicals knew
and spoke very little about the "living God who deals
familiarly with men". The Doctor said on this score,
"Brethren, we are mad, mad! " ',[60] As a result, 'when this
element of spiritual life which was the result of the working of the Holy Spirit was under consideration, the
Doctor could beome a critic of orthodoxy, even
Reformed orthodoxy'. Some exponents of Reformed
theology were 'overlooking or excluding the immediate
works of the Spirit in addition to regeneration, viz, the
baptism of the Spirit, the bestowal of spiritual gifts, and
revival'.[61]

As Iain Murray has pointed out, a concern for a great
outpouring of the Spirit in revival power was at the heart
of the Doctor's theology, and influenced, as we shall see,
his ecclesiology as well. As Jim Packer has shown, in his
theology of revival, the Doctor was far closer to the great
American eighteenth-century leader Jonathan Edwards
than he was to the Puritans—Edwards held to what
Packer has described as a cyclical view. He certainly saw
revival himself in the American colonies as it can be said
that the Doctor saw revival in his early years in Aberavon.

To the Doctor, the fact that Warfield, that great
Reformed expositor, did not believe in the continuation
of spiritual gifts was 'a new form of dispensationalism'.
Jonathan Edwards had distinguished between excesses
and the truly spiritual, or, as he told the ministers at
the Fellowhip, 'We must learn to draw the line between
the essential and the indifferent on the one hand, and on
the other between the indifferent and the wrong.'[62] His
own wife and brother-in-law had themselves seen the most
extraordinary phenomena in the 1904–5 revival in Wales,
to which their father had sent them, so the Doctor was

well aware of some of the more unusual occurrences from members of his own family.

As a result, Hywel Jones writes, the 'Doctor was interested in anything which appeared to display signs of spiritual vitality'.[63] When issues of charismatic theology and practice came up in discussion

> the Doctor was most careful. He would not discuss all such phenomena as psychological or demonic, as some would have preferred. But he did not hesitate to say that those elements could be present. On the other hand, he would not and did not endorse the charismatic movement *per se*. He urged careful observation and evaluation in the light of what the Bible taught of the spiritual effects of an experience of God— awe and reverence, a sense of personal sin and unworthiness, love to the Saviour and the brethren, concern for the perishing and a spirit of prayer. His most emphatic charge directed against us was, 'Why do we not have problems associated with spiritual life?' and the answer was obvious.[64]

So while he did not urge ministers to follow charismatic practice, he did call on them to 'seek the Lord without setting limits on what he might do or what we would allow him to do, asking him to turn to us and visit us in gracious revival'.[65]

That is surely it, of course. It shows the heart of the man, the reason behind everything he thought and did.

In addition, the Doctor showed that many in the church had had the baptism with the Holy Spirit, but as it had been called by another name, people had not recognised it for what it was. Jim Packer makes the same point in *Keep in Step with the Spirit*. So often people agree fully on key doctrinal issues, but maintain that they do not because their terminology is different. The writer Donald Bridge has a classic example in his book *Power Evangelism and the Word of God*, where he describes two churches that insisted they had different theologies on divine healing today. One believed in it, but the other, while claiming that it did not, none the less saw many people healed. How was this, given their theology? Well, they both believed in answered prayer!

This shows how ridiculous much of the discussion was. It also reveals that the Reformed constituency got into a mess because it allowed the charismatics to determine the terminology. If they said that the experience separate from conversion was called baptism with the Holy Spirit, and they believed that that had to include certain things, then when the Doctor also said that baptism with the Holy Spirit was separate from conversion, this fact had to be denied or attacked, because of what the charismatics meant by the term.

The Doctor used the same words, but, as we have seen, meant something different by them—a sealing of the Spirit, power not to do unusual things but power for witness, to spread the good news of Jesus Christ. He used the terms not because others did, but because he found them in Scripture, and that was enough for him! Whereas many of his Reformed friends were entirely reactive in their approach, he was innovative and proactive.

As we have seen, his views on the Holy Spirit exposed the fact that people who wanted to call themselves his closest disciples often disagreed with him on key issues, and when *Joy Unspeakable* was published, this became very apparent with one side, and the same for the other side when the caveats in *Prove All Things* (*The Sovereign Spirit*) came out not long later. (One interesting observation—the more controversial *Joy Unspeakable* has outsold by a large margin its more cautious companion volume. Maybe those who wanted to believe in the baptism with the Holy Spirit without qualification did not want to know of the equally biblical restraints! One trusts not—and of course controversy always sells more than caution. The two books form one sermon series, and happily now they have been reunited in one volume.)

One of the big problems was the game of false logical consequences. The Doctor alluded to this in his sermon, which we saw earlier, when he said that people would say that if one believed in the baptism with the Holy Spirit, one had to believe in speaking in tongues. Part of the problem, as Jim Packer has pointed out, is that we do not tackle the issues properly. People on the Reformed side seemed to think that if Calvin did not believe in baptism with the Spirit as a separate experience, nor should they. This was of course to elevate Calvin to a position higher than Scripture! As we have seen, ultimately if Calvin said one thing and the Bible said another, Calvin was wrong. To the Doctor, this was not a problem, but to many who had discovered the glorious truths that Calvin had also discovered in Scripture, with all their liberating power, then it was a shock to find that he could be wrong. Instinctively, and in human terms understandably, they rebelled against the notion. It is much easier to believe in a simple package than to sift through everything and seemingly believe three contradictory things before breakfast!

However, if the charismatics thought the Doctor believed their package, they were, as we have seen, equally mistaken. One can see their enthusiasm too. As a charismatic friend in the USA, a Presbyterian, once said to me, he was amazed when he heard that 'Mr Reformed', the Doctor, believed in the baptism with the Holy Spirit. This was of enormous encouragement to him, as it showed that one could have this extraordinary experience of blessing from the Lord and be Reformed at the same time!

But of course the Doctor meant something entirely different by the term than classic charismatic or pentecostal theology. Many 'Reformed charismatics' saw this and took his view. Many charismatics, through discovering the Doctor's work, became Reformed. What many people in the Reformed wing of the church saw as the nightmare of defections from their own to the charismatic camp was unnecessary when one thinks that many charismatics joined the Reformed wing of Evangelicalism as a result of Dr Lloyd-Jones.

So what of those who in the charismatic camp felt encouraged by the Doctor? What of those like the Anglican charismatics Michael Harper and the late David Watson, both of whom have written most warmly of his encouragement? The same applies to New Frontiers leader Terry Virgo and one of his leading lieutenants, Henry Tyler; also to the late Arthur Wallis, and to the founder of Ichthus, Roger Forster, who is not only charismatic but a passionately convinced Arminian. All of these men have written of the encouragement he gave them. It still amazes me that people are perturbed when they hear that the Doctor met or influenced certain people of other theological persuasions. They should be glad! When my book *Five Evangelical Leaders* came out in 1984, with a chapter on Dr Lloyd-Jones, a review in a much respected Reformed journal concentrated on the casual remark that Terry Virgo had met the Doctor. This worried the reviewer as he was afraid this might imply endorsement of Terry Virgo's views of apostolic ministry in the church today, failing perhaps to see the conversely encouraging factor that Terry's theology is in fact Calvinistic in much of its perspective.

We need to remember what Hywel Jones said earlier—the Doctor was in favour of life. Many charismatic churches had such life. As the Doctor says in *Joy Unspeakable* on the problems of excess:

Look at the New Testament church, and you see it vibrant with a spiritual life, and, of course, it is always life that tends to lead to excesses. There is no problem of discipline in a graveyard . . . Problems are created by life and by vigour, and the problems of the early church were spiritual problems, problems arising because of the danger of going to excess in the spiritual realm.[66]

In other words, these churches had life! Of course this did not mean that the Doctor endorsed everything these people believed. For example, as we will see, the Doctor was to fall out drastically with Anglican Evangelicals. Likewise, the fact that the Doctor gladly received both Terry Virgo and Arthur Wallis does not mean an endorsement of their views on church structure. (This is ironic in many ways as there are plenty of people who feel that although he would certainly never have said so himself, the only real way in which to describe the Doctor's ministry, especially in the last years of his life, is precisely apostolic!)

But if people had life, and came to him for general support and Christian fellowship, then he would always want to encourage them. As he would say to folk, 'Keep on! Keep on!' Sometimes his judgement of people was faulty and he let his enthusiasm carry him away and get the better of him. But this was not a cause for concern in the family. Mrs Lloyd-Jones may not have had all the theological acumen of her husband, nor would she ever have claimed to, but when it came to assessing people, her mind was razor sharp, and she always saw through anything or anyone dubious. She was, of course, the epitome of politeness to visitors. But when they were gone, the family—and of course the Doctor himself—soon knew what she thought!

However, the main thing about the Doctor is that he never thought in man-made categories. If you believe X,

then it follows that you believe Y and Z too. 'No! No!' as
he often used to say in his sermons. If the Scripture says to
believe X, A and K, then that is fine. If a Christian brother
had life, and believed the Scripture on the person and
work of Christ, then if he believed X, that was fine!
Encouraging life in his church did not mean an endorsement of Y and Z, and, in due time, if there was real life
continuing in the church, then they would soon come to
believe A and K as well. But better a man who believed X,
W and R than one who believed all the right things, but
who had a church that was lifeless. Lifeless churches were
no honour to God and that is what counted.

As Bob Horn, the UCCF General Secretary, has written
in *His Place in Evangelicalism*, many sides wished to
claim the Doctor exclusively for themselves. Like all truly
great men, he suffered from his disciples! Some admitted
that he had a view different from their own, but, as Bob
Horn puts it, 'Some erstwhile disciples became a shade
condescending.' But the truth was that while

> many claimed him, none owned him. The Gospel Lion was
> no one's pet. He had a far bigger mind and heart than any
> who play him up or put him down . . . He was not the captive
> of any group or 'ism' or school or movement. He was bigger
> than them all. That was his greatness . . . He was Christ-
> centred and saw all else from that perspective. He had a sense
> of proportion, a sense of timing, a sense of history, a sense of
> God . . . [67]

'Spiritual life' . . . 'a sense of God'. These were what
counted, rather than wrangles about what Calvin said,
or what some Puritan may or may not have written. Since
his death the battle lines have changed much anyway, with
many charismatics coming to realise their true evangelical
roots—perhaps, as Jim Packer has said, more so in Britain
than in the USA, but that might change too. People who

never spoke to each other in the Doctor's lifetime are now discovering their common evangelical heritage. He never saw the revival for which he so longed, and at the time of writing it has still not come. But when it does, surely he will be seen as a forerunner, proclaiming in advance from Scripture the message of the kind of Christians we all need to be. May his dream come true!

8

Unity and Schism
1966

Background

By 1966, the Doctor's thinking on the subject of the church was crystallising. Although it was not essentially changed from his earlier views, it was undergoing a change of emphasis in that he now brought what he had long thought to the forefront, and made it into a key issue—something that he was to do with increasing vigour for the rest of his life.

In the 1950s he published *Maintaining the Evangelical Faith Today*, based on a talk given to the InterVarsity Fellowship in 1952. It is a good summary of his doctrinal position and of his view of the church—the key issue to the post-1966 debate. He was, he told his IVF audience, 'by nature a pacific person', but despite that one who felt obliged to be controversial because of the growing challenge of the ecumenical movement. (He and Francis Schaeffer had had some good talks on this only a few years before, when the two men expressed their grave concerns to one another—the Doctor's worries in 1952 were of long standing.) In particular, the ecumenism fostered by the World Council of Churches posed a real problem to doctrinal purity.

Consequently, Evangelicals were being called upon increasingly to defend their position, not out of any kind of partisan spirit—as we saw in his talks with Shields back in the 1930s, he always opposed that kind of attitude—but because the Bible itself gave them no alternative. Christians had to be clear on who Christ was and on why he had come. This meant that they sometimes ended up being accused of intolerance—but such, of course, had been the fate of Martin Luther before them.

God demanded faith in himself and obedience, and therefore the kind of compromises that some were making were unacceptable. *Biblical* unity, as shown in the Book of Acts and in the Epistles, was always on the basis of 'doctrine and fellowship', centred on Christ. Evangelicals should therefore separate themselves from those who were preaching 'another gospel'.

However, they should only split on matters 'absolutely essential' to the truth, not on issues such as baptism or doctrines of the millennium. They should also be careful to watch what men did *not* say, as all real Christians were bound to preach certain things sooner or later. The evangelical faith was nothing new, but was historical; the one on which all Evangelicals ought to be abundantly clear themselves.

The IVF was of course in itself a group of differing denominations, from Baptist through to Anglican and consisting of Evangelicals in groups that were entirely evangelical to denominations like the more theologically liberal Congregational Union, of which Westminster Chapel was still a member. With the evangelical Anglicans, there was no doubt that at this stage their primary self-identification was as *Evangelicals* who were also Anglican—something that would be very important later.

The Doctor had also been instrumental in drawing up a statement on the doctrinal distinctives of IFES—at the time he was the Chairman, and in 1966 he remained the

President. On the issue of the nature of the church, the statement reads:

> The church of Christ consists of all those who in all ages have been or are in vital relationship with our Lord Jesus Christ as a result of the new birth. The New Testament itself recognises only two aspects of the church: (1) the whole company of believers in heaven and on earth; and (2) the local manifestation which is the gathering in fellowship of all who are in Christ and, in the midst of whom, according to his promises, Christ is present, who is the only Lord and head of the church.[68]

In other words, the church consisted of all true believing Christians quite regardless of any kind of denominational background. Indeed the true church as such did not believe in or recognise them. As we have seen, in a grouping as interdenominational as IFES this was very important.

However, the main thing about these statements is that they are wholly positive. They make abundantly clear what it is that Evangelicals believe. They also make it plain that biblical, Christ-centred truth is the basis of fellowship among Christians—something which completely transcends man-made edifices such as denominations.

What they do not address is what Evangelicals do about denominations, and what an Evangelical should do in a denomination in which there are people, leaders even, who do not believe these things and maybe even preach against them.

Of course, the logical inference is clear. 'You are an Evangelical?'

'Yes!'

'But your bishop thinks that Evangelicals are a bunch of simpletons who distort the gospel, and a professor in one of your seminaries has denied the Virgin Birth.'

'Yes, of course, but the basis of faith of my denomination (the Thirty-Nine Articles) affirms the centrality and truth both of the atonement and of the Virgin Birth. . . .'

One can see the argument coming!

Crossing the Rubicon

This very dilemma had been coming increasingly apparent to the Doctor. He had long been of the opinion that true Evangelicals could not really remain loyal to their biblical, evangelical position and at the same time cheerfully be active in a denomination with those who openly denied basic gospel truths. The way in which Evangelicals could stay in what one might call 'doctrinally mixed denominations' was to his logical mind completely illogical! Many of them had solved the problem by ignoring it. Many a vicar ignored his liberal or exceedingly high church bishop, or concentrated, in terms of fellowship, with other Evangelicals either inside or outside the denomination, such as through the IVF, while ignoring the minister in their own denomination in the town next door who rejected basic biblical truths in every sermon. (It is important to realise, in view of later misunderstanding, that the Doctor did not ever become 'anti-Anglican' per se. It was simply that in England, the Church of England was by far the biggest of the 'mixed' denominations.)

During the nearly forty years he had been in the ministry so far, he had not made the doctrine of the church something of key importance. Now he felt that things were going too far, and that the situation had to be addressed. The drift could not continue. By 1966 he felt that the threat posed by the lowest common denominator approach of the World Council of Churches, many of whose members and groups denied basic doctrines of the Christian faith, had grown too deep. He could not

see how Evangelicals could in all clear Christian conscience remain in denominations that were affiliated to
the WCC.

That year there had been talk in the Evangelical
Alliance of a united evangelical denomination, and a
commission had been set up to examine the issue—the
Doctor had been one of the witnesses to it. Not surprisingly, the feeling had been that there was no demand for
such a group.

In October 1966 the Evangelical Alliance decided to
have a meeting of its National Evangelical Assembly. Dr
Lloyd-Jones was asked to speak on the first night, the
18th. He therefore chose to use the opportunity of this
meeting in the Westminster Central Hall to share his
current thinking. All of us in the family knew that it
would be historic and my mother told me that I had to
come as what my grandfather was going to say would be
vitally important. So there I was, a small eleven-year-old
boy, in the balcony!

The EA leadership knew full well what the Doctor was
going to say, and, as his old friend Leith Samuel has
written, they were also fully aware that his statement
was going to be very controversial! However, what none
of us could know was that it would turn out to be what
many have since called his 'Rubicon'. Nor did anyone
guess what the effect would be of putting in the chair
the revered and highly-respected Anglican Evangelical,
John Stott, including Stott himself.

The Doctor began by saying that it was time Evangelicals faced up to the issues raised by the biblical doctrine
of the church. Too often, it seemed to him, they appeared
'more concerned to maintain the integrity of their
denominations than anyone else'. The growing power
and influence of the ecumenical movement made this
issue more crucial than it had been before.

As a result, there were two urgent issues. First, were Evangelicals prepared to be no more than a wing of their respective denominations? Secondly, what exactly was the true Christian church? Evangelicals, he felt, 'rightly put doctrine before fellowship'. The church was made up of the saints, and for true Christians to insist on staying in different denominations was, in effect therefore, to be guilty of the sin of schism.

This is something particularly important to note, because there have been many since who have tried to accuse the Doctor of this very crime! Yet the irony is, his point was that the prime fellowship is of necessity with other biblical believers, and that to maintain distinctives not based on Scripture is actually to divide God's people.

Consequently, he argued, the need for the 'ancient witness' as shown by the Reformers had never been stronger. Only by standing together could Evangelicals expect the Holy Spirit to send them revival. (We shall soon see what he meant by this.)

There would be difficulties to face for those who left their mixed denominations. But Christians, the faithful remnant, need never fear, as the Bible made clear. Evangelicals should 'rise to the occasion and listen to the call of God'. If they had only one objective—the glory of God—they would be 'led by the Spirit to the true answer', which was to leave their mixed denominations.

It is also vital to mention that his basic message was not so much a negative one—*leave*—but a positive one: *join together* as God's people. This again is important to remember as folklore grows on what he actually said! (The full text appears in two books: *Knowing the Times* published by the Banner of Truth and *The Best of Martyn Lloyd-Jones* published by Kingsway.)

As he himself said:

I am a believer in ecumenicity, evangelical ecumenicity. . . .
You and I have been called to a positive task . . . We shall
need great grace. We shall need to be filled with the Spirit. We
shall all need to be humble. . . And who knows but that the
ecumenical movement may be something for which, in years
to come, we shall thank God because it made us face our
problems on the church level, instead of on the level of
movements, and really brought us together as a fellowship
or an association of evangelical churches. May God speed the
day![69]

This in itself was strong stuff! However, the atmosphere
was charged still further by the way in which the remarks
of the Chairman, John Stott, were received. Even as a boy
of eleven I could see that something dramatic was happening! Stott has put it thus: he thanked the Doctor for his
talk, and then 'with much nervousness and diffidence'
made a few words in reply. Unfortunately for John Stott,
they came over far more forcefully than he had intended.
What he said was: 'I believe history is against what Dr
Lloyd-Jones has said . . . Scripture is against him . . . I
hope no one will act precipitately. . . We are all concerned
with the same ultimate issues and with the glory of God.'[70]

Later on, John Stott was to apologise to the Doctor for
unwittingly creating such an atmosphere in the Hall. As
Stott has written in a tribute to the Doctor, the two men
'continued to have a warm personal relationship'.[71] When
the Doctor was in hospital two years later, John Stott
went out of his way to be kind both to him and to Mrs
Lloyd-Jones; something that is sadly not as well known as
it should be. But at the time, the atmosphere was electric!
John Stott was clearly worried that many an impression-
able young evangelical Anglican would leave the Church
of England forthwith! This was entirely understandable
from his point of view. But neither he nor the Doctor
could have foreseen the result of the limited interchange.

Many Anglicans at the time showed that they rather misunderstood what the Doctor had *actually* said. Michael Saward has written in *Evangelicals on the Move* that he had asked 'Anglican Evangelicals to leave their compromised church and join him in a pure Reformed Church. He got a dusty answer, delivered publicly, by John Stott'.[72] David Winter wrote in *Life of Faith* at the time that 'Dr Martyn Lloyd-Jones made an eloquent plea to evangelicals to leave their denominations and join a United Evangelical Church'.[73]

What he really said . . . and why

Both were wrong because the Doctor never even considered anything of the kind. It never occurred to him to set up an evangelical denomination, as he knew that such a beast was completely impossible anyway. Furthermore, as Iain Murray has correctly pointed out in his official biography, organisation was something to which the Doctor was entirely alien. The very thought of it was foreign to him.

What he really wanted was a kind of loose affiliation, on the lines of the FIEC. This would not be a denomination—with constituent members as diverse as the Free Presbyterians and the Strict Baptists, this would not have been realistic, and the Doctor knew that. He had in mind something of a confederation, where all the denominations within it would maintain their distinctives, but which one had to be firmly evangelical to join.

This loose grouping would also act as a voice on behalf of Evangelicals, especially those in smaller denominations or causes. (Ironically, the EA in the 1990s is trying to do something not unlike this, with the Doctor's own son-in-law, Fred Catherwood, as its President, so that part of the Doctor's vision is being fulfilled at last.) Membership of

this confederation would convey a seal of doctrinal
approval to basic evangelical tenets of faith, so that while
the confederation member might be FIEC in one town,
Strict Baptist in another, a completely independent church
in yet another, anyone coming to that town wanting an
authentically evangelical church would know they were
safe. That is not to say that a local Baptist Union or
Anglican church could not also be evangelical and faithful to the gospel. But whereas simply being Baptist was
not itself a guarantee, a link to this wider confederation
would be.

The Anglican, J. I. Packer, had a better understanding
of the situation than Michael Saward and David Winter.
As we have seen, he and the Doctor had been close for
twenty years, especially through their mutual devotion to
Puritan theology. Packer has described the Doctor in
Chosen Vessels thus: 'He was the greatest man I have
ever known . . . I know that much of my vision today is
what it is because he was what he was, and his influence
has no doubt gone deeper than I can trace.'[74]

Needless to say, as Jim Packer was staying within the
Church of England, this issue was to cause a tragic rift
between the two men, though, as Packer has written on
their disagreement, 'Was either of us right? History will
judge, and to history I remit the matter.'[75]

But on the substantive issue of what the Doctor was
trying to do, Jim Packer has made it clear in *A Kind of
Puritan* that he fully understood that the Doctor had no
intention of being divisive or of trying to set up a new
denomination.

Packer writes:

He never gave substance to his vision by producing, or getting
others to produce, a blueprint for the new para-denomina-
tion . . . Probably the truest thing to say about his campaign

of words without plans is that he was testing the waters, looking to see if the Holy Spirit would use what he said to evoke major support and a widespread desire for action, and he would not risk prejudicing his own prophetic role in the process by any appearance of wanting to be a denominational boss. And who will blame him for that?[76]

He had, as Packer realised, no wish to be any kind of boss of anything. Furthermore, as Dr Packer has written in the same piece, it was the Puritan at the heart of the Doctor that led him to do as he did; above all with the Puritan longing for true revival burning at the centre. Revival! That was the thing for which the Doctor longed above all. He was not interested in committees or structures. What he wanted was a mighty outpouring of the Spirit of God! Packer has called him an 'eighteenth-century man', by which he means someone who yearns for the power of God in the land that was seen in the days of George Whitefield or Jonathan Edwards. Above all else, his desire for a pure church is one that should be seen in that light, and that is how we should understand what he was saying in 1966.

The aftermath

Many did follow the Doctor, yet this is often forgotten, because people have concentrated on the Anglicans, very few of whom did leave (and the best known, Herbert Carson, was in fact technically Church of Ireland). He gave considerable care to those who did come out, as he felt pastorally responsible for them. One of them was Vernon Higham of Cardiff, who came out of the Presby-terian Church of Wales. (A wonderful irony that has been pointed out recently by Wyn James of the Evangelical Press of Wales in a letter to the *Evangelical Times*, is that *the Doctor himself never left this denomination*!

Whether by design or not, we do not know, but it is in fact true.) Vernon Higham was later to reciprocate this great kindness by being like an honorary son to Mrs Lloyd-Jones in the ten years between the Doctor's death and her own. He rang her every Sunday night to see how she was. Whenever she was with us in the family home in Balsham, the telephone would ring as we were eating our meal after the evening service. Without even picking it up, we would say, 'Gu'—the Welsh word we used for her— 'it's Vernon Higham!' We were invariably right!

Obviously many things needed sorting out, and one of them was the fraternal of ministers, which had been interdenominational since it began in 1943. So a small group of people close to the Doctor gathered with him to work out an official statement. What they said is important, not just for what they did say but equally for what they did *not* say.

In the statement, they made it very clear that they recognised that 'all conservative Evangelicals do not see eye to eye with us over the issues' and that it was perfectly possible to be a true Christian while remaining in a doctrinally mixed denomination. The Doctor would never accuse anyone who disagreed with him on this issue of ceasing to be an Evangelical, however mistaken he felt that person's doctrine of the church to be.

Some Anglicans remained friends regardless. One of them, ironically, was John Gwynn Thomas, a wonderfully genial Welshman who succeeded Herbert Carson to a church in Cambridge when Carson withdrew from his vicarage in response to the Doctor's call. Perhaps that friendship provides an important clue. Thomas was Welsh, and the Doctor was, as we know, Welsh to the core. That Welshness is important, because it reveals, as some have perceived, why the Doctor never really understood why the Anglican Evangelicals did not secede. To him, it was a doctrinal issue, and that was an end of it! But to the Anglicans, they were leaving the national church, part of what being English was all about! There was a very real sense in which they would have felt less English if they had left—the whole theology of 'the church in one place', by which the local Anglican church is not just any old church but *the* church in that place, because of its status as the Established Church in the life of the nation.

The Wittenberg Anniversary

As time passed, the Doctor was able to develop his ideas. He spoke in Westminster Chapel in 1967 to commemorate the 450th anniversary of Luther's famous nailing of the 95 Theses to the door of the church in Wittenberg.

Again, my family felt that his talk would be historic, so as a twelve-year-old boy, I sat at the back of the church, all attention. On this occasion my sister Bethan and brother Jonathan were also present. Jonathan, aged six, was rather puzzled. He turned to my mother and said, 'Mum, is today Sunday?'

'No,' replied my mother, 'it's Wednesday.'

'Well,' said Jonathan, 'if it's Wednesday, then what am I doing in church?!'

The Doctor had been worried, he told us, about the increasing strength of the ecumenical movement. He was also very worried about the recent Anglican Congress at Keele. It was, he felt, 'impossible' for an 'Evangelical to be yoked together with others in the church who deny the very elements of Christian faith'. Evangelicals who remained in doctrinally mixed groupings were, he felt, 'virtually saying that though you think you are right, they may also be right', both in their doctrine and in their interpretation of Scripture. 'That,' he proclaimed to us, 'is a denial of the Evangelical, the only true faith.' The idea put forward by leading Evangelicals in the Church of England that Evangelicals could, by staying in doctrinally mixed denominations, reform them and return them to evangelical faith was, to him, 'midsummer madness'. There was no hope of such a transformation taking place. For him there was only one option for Evangelicals, and that was to heed John's words in Revelation 18:4, 'Come out of her my people!'[77]

But, as always, he ended on a positive note. He urged them to 'come into fellowship with all like-minded Christian people'. As the private memorandum quoted earlier put it, this would be 'together on an uncompromising gospel basis', with those whose 'first loyalty' was to the 'conservative evangelical faith, rather than to any inherited traditional position'.[78]

Part of the problem was that to some evangelical Anglicans, like Jim Packer, their prime loyalty *was* to the 'conservative Evangelical faith'. As he has written in *Chosen Vessels*, 'In continuing to combat error, commend truth and strengthen evangelical ministry as best I could in the Church of England, he [the Doctor] thought I was showing myself a denominationalist and obstructing evangelical unity, besides being caught in a hopelessly compromised position. By contrast, I believed that the claims of evangelical unity do not require ecclesiastical separation where the faith is not actually being denied and renewal remains possible,' and that in asking for Evangelicals to leave their denominations for a wider unity it was thus the Doctor who 'was the denominationalist'.[79]

The areas of disagreement and the different ways of thinking are therefore clear! He had a very clear vision of a gloriously united Evangelicalism, with the gospel of Jesus Christ placed firmly at the centre. To him, the fact that Evangelicals were divided by man-made barriers was tragic. Obviously, they would disagree on other, lesser issues. The British Evangelical Council, to which he now became all the closer, had among its constituent members Free Presbyterians from Scotland, who believed in infant baptism, and Grace Baptists, who believed that only professing Christians should ever be baptised, and by full immersion. Clearly, these divisions would not go away. But the point is that these were exclusively *evangelical* groupings, united with other Evangelicals, and who were all united on the basics of the faith. It is not, therefore, that he was *against* people or groups, but that he was *for* evangelical unity.

Unfortunately, many in 'mixed' denominations felt as we have seen that his view was essentially negative. It would be abandoning any hope, which they still nurtured, of reclaiming their denominations, many of which, like the Church of England with its Thirty-nine Articles, had bases of faith which were thoroughly biblical, even though many, if not most, of the denomination had long ceased to believe it.

Keele and after

Of course many Anglicans did not—and still do not—believe that they are a denomination. As the Canadian theologian, D. A. Carson, has said, to a Welshman like the Doctor, the whole concept of a State or Established Church was quite alien—indeed we knew in the family that he found it a bizarre notion quite alien to Scripture. So the divide expanded.

The other major event in 1967 was the National Evangelical Anglican Congress at Keele. This strongly affirmed the desire of Evangelicals in the Church of England to affirm their Anglican heritage and work more closely within the denominational framework. One of the visitors, looking on approvingly, was the Archbishop of Canterbury, Michael Ramsey—someone who had been very critical of Evangelicalism during the 1950s.

As John Stott put it in *Keele '67*: 'Evangelicals in the Church of England are changing too. Not in doctrinal conviction (for the truth of the gospel cannot change), but (like any healthy child) in stature and posture.' Indeed, he commented of his fellow Anglican Evangelicals, 'We have acquired a reputation for narrow partisanship and obstructionism.' Evangelicals in the Church of England 'need to repent and change'.[80]

Consequently, the official statement declared: 'We have been slow to learn from other parts of God's Church . . . The initial task for divided Christians is dialogue at all levels and across all barriers. We desire to enter this ecumenical dialogue fully. . . .'[81]

Many of the Doctor's followers have regarded this as vindication for their view. 'There you are. We knew all along!' However, events in the Church of England in the 1990s have shown that there are many in the Church of England whose prime loyalty is *not* to the denomination, but to Scripture and other vital evangelical truths. While not all may agree with them on every issue—many argue that one can take a very conservative view of Scripture and combine it with women's ministry, for example—it is being said in many circles of the Church of England that Keele was not necessarily a helpful thing. It deflected Evangelicals into ecclesiastical politics and took many a good man away from the prime tasks of ministry, like preaching the gospel.

The main point too about such a move today is that it is coming from *within* the Church of England itself; from Evangelicals who wonder what their espousal of evangelical truth means in terms of membership of an Established Church which has to be, by definition, comprehensive. Several leading Anglican Evangelicals are wondering how long they can stay in, and have told their congregations as much. Many Evangelicals practise things on Sundays which they believe to be biblical, but which are technically against Canon Law. In some dioceses, the bishop might wink (the evangelical parish is probably one of the biggest in the diocese and funds much of the diocese's work through the diocesan quota). But not all bishops are so sympathetic, and ironically bishops appointed from evangelical backgrounds are often very tough in an effort to show no favouritism.

Once again, though, the point is that the logic of the position is working its way through *from within*. The main problem of 1966 is that it was seen as something imposed *from without*, from someone who had never been an Anglican. Although 1966 was never intended to be as dramatic as it turned out to be, the accidental appearance of a clash between two of Britain's leading Evangelicals—Lloyd-Jones and Stott—forced something in a way which turned out to be very unhelpful. If it was an appeal for biblical unity that was meant to restore rather than to rend asunder, it came too forcefully for many a vicar of the time. It was an appeal made too soon.

Francis Schaeffer, the great thinker, was himself part of a separated denomination; someone who had in fact left a doctrinally mixed grouping as far back as the 1930s. (Os Guiness once told me that Francis Schaeffer and Martyn Lloyd-Jones were two men *par excellence* who, if they had lived during the Reformation, would have gone to the stake for their beliefs!) So on that point, he was very much at one with the view the Doctor took in 1966.

However, Schaeffer tackled it differently. Instead of attacking the problem *structurally*, he tackled it *doctrinally*. Now the Doctor thought he was tackling it doctrinally himself! But what Schaeffer did was to attack the beliefs of those in mixed denominations, making the implications crystal clear. For example, sensing the dangers in where Evangelicalism was heading, he told the Lausanne Congress of World Evangelism in 1974 that 'inerrancy is the watershed of Evangelicalism'. The Doctor would have agreed fully with this, but so of course does J. I. Packer, who stayed in the Church of England, and has been one of the most passionate defenders of biblical inerrancy for over twenty years.

Furthermore, Schaeffer also realised two dangers. First, those who stay inside a denomination shift the line beyond which they will not go. The thing that propels them out always gets worse and worse, but often the ultimate point never arrives! By contrast, those who do pull out can become very harsh and unloving, looking judgementally on those who have remained within.

Sadly, as the positions polarised, the gap between fellow Evangelicals within and without did widen—the old friendship between Martyn Lloyd-Jones and J. I. Packer being one of the casualties. (Though as we will see later, this did not affect Dr Packer's relationship with other members of the family, which remained open and warm.)

This parting pulled the rug from under the Evangelicals within the Church of England whose primary identity remained their Evangelicalism and not their Anglicanism. Their love and admiration for the Doctor continued, albeit from a distance. But as the Doctor's followers increasingly refused to have anything to do with them, they lost the alliance of fellow Evangelicals on key issues.

As has been said, there is an extent to which the Doctor was responsible for Keele. There is surely a lot in this view. By creating a polarity, albeit for the best of reasons, the Doctor split Evangelicalism and created the very schism that he was so anxious to avoid. If fellowship with Evangelicals in other denominations was now cut off, as increasingly became the case, many an Evangelical inside a mixed denomination concentrated on fellowship within his own denomination, whether the others were Evangelicals or not.

As Bob Horn has put it in his very perceptive essay, 'His Place in Evangelicalism': 'The evangelical scene has not been the same since.' He argues:

> Before 1966, evangelicals had been more conscious of their ties to each other than their links to denominations . . . we were in general militantly defensive—battling for the truth against the ecumenical monoliths, with a simple clarity and a robust cohesion. After 1966, evangelicalism drifted into various camps . . . denominational affairs took up time and energy that could have (and previously had) gone to inter-evangelical relationships. Evangelicals, denominational and independent, drifted apart.[82]

Horn makes clear that in mixed denominations, the Doctor's influence dropped, which was inevitable, and that ties in with an experience I had when the Doctor came to speak to the Oxford Inter-Collegiate Christian Union, OICCU. There was now a generation 'that knew not Joseph'! This was true of my Anglican contemporaries in the OICCU. They thought that the Doctor, like Spurgeon, was a great nineteenth-century figure, long dead. So they were amazed that not only was he my grandfather but very much still alive! None of them had ever heard him preach before, and as one of them said to me in pleasant amazement, 'Your grandfather, Christopher, wasn't half bad!' (The President of OICCU, Lindsay Brown, was a Welshman, and knew full well who he was! The Doctor was to be a great encouragement to him, and Lindsay Brown is now the General Secretary of the IFES.)

In his own circles he inevitably became even more influential; too much so in many ways. He certainly never saw himself as a kind of guru figure to be quoted—the idea was abhorrent to him! But to many he became like a talisman—'the Doctor says' becoming a phrase to end all argument. (This device was even used against his own grandson in many a student discussion! Thankfully I knew he preferred me to come to my own conclusions from Scripture, as he did everyone else.) As so often happens, people gave him their own prejudices, ascribing views to him that he never held. Sometimes this was farcical: the Doctor was strongly teetotal, especially after seeing the devastating effect of alcohol in Aberavon. But I remember being told, very categorically, that the Doctor often enjoyed a small tipple before a sermon!

This hardening did not help inter-evangelical relationships. As was seen earlier, the private statement drawn up by the Doctor and others in the Westminster Fraternal made it clear that it was perfectly possible to be a conservative Evangelical and be within a mixed denomination—however incomprehensible and regrettable that might be. So private fellowship was still possible. But soon the mood hardened. Some would not have fellowship of any kind with anyone in a mixed denomination— what one might call second-degree separation. Others went even further still. They would not have fellowship with anyone *in a separated denomination* who had fellowship with those in one that was still doctrinally mixed— what one might call third-degree separation. I am not sure whether there are those who go further still—and have no fellowship with those who do not have fellowship with those in mixed denominations, but who do have fellowship within their own separated denominations with those who do!

As Bob Horn has so accurately observed, the 'state of independent evangelicalism since 1966 has not been all that he [the Doctor] encouraged it and urged it to be. It became clear that not all the blame for evangelical divisions lay the other side of the watershed' of 1966. 'Independents were prone to subdivide and did not always keep a sense of proportion when they differed from each other. Little empires tended to form. Those who urged secession seldom tried to make their own grass greener than it was on the denominational side . . . The separatist camp often looked uninviting to any would-be seceder.'[83]

Sadly the Doctor did not do all he could to rein in the more aggressive and possibly hot-headed zealots on his own side. With his love of history and encyclopaedic knowledge of the seventeenth century, it is surprising that he did not know from past experience what might happen to his own followers. When he died, and was no longer there to contradict, some of those followers tended to be very dogmatic about what he would and would not have said, always quoting him as being on their own side. Ironically, some of them were anti-Catholic, yet their method of quoting the Doctor as some infallible source reminded some of us strongly of unreformed Catholic appeals to tradition and the invocation of the saints!

Fortunately, as Bob Horn has written, some

in the inclusive denominations, however, came to see that triumphalism is one thing, the triumph of the truth quite another. A more biblical realism emerged. They became more aware of who and where their true friends were. At the same time, some outside such bodies came to see that a church which is uncompromised doctrinally can be compromised

just as seriously in other ways; and that cold or dead orthodoxy is of little use to God or man.[84]

In other words, it is gospel unity that matters. One of the
biggest problems posed by some of the Doctor's followers
is that they make his views entirely static—and he is no
longer around to say otherwise! But as we have seen in the
chapter on *Joy Unspeakable*, he came to shift his views on
several subjects, from the 'Man in Romans 7'—is he or is
he not a Christian?—to the whole question of the baptism
with the Holy Spirit. Evangelicalism has changed a lot
too, both in Britain and the USA. Many of the New
Churches in Britain have become very strong, and have
a separated ecclesiology. Some of them are even more
divisive than anyone else, while others will cheerfully
work alongside Evangelicals from other groups. The
Evangelical Alliance is profoundly different from what it
was thirty years ago, with a strong welcome to Reformed
Evangelicals and a passionate belief among much of the
top leadership in key issues such as inerrancy. Indeed it is
now *very* different, as the President appointed in 1992 was
none other than the Doctor's own son-in-law, Frederick
Catherwood, whose passionate evangelical convictions
fully match the Doctor's own.

A yearning for revival

One can speculate what the Doctor would have made of it
all, and on how he would have reacted to the great debates
going on within Anglican Evangelicalism, itself now
becoming less monolithic the more it fragments. But the
main point is surely that he would not have wanted us to
speculate. We are called to be faithful to God *for our own
generation*. We do not know what God has in store for the
future. God's truth is eternal, but our world changes, so

we have to think what the biblical reaction is to things *now*. Who in 1988 could have predicted the quite extraordinary events of 1989, let alone from the vantage point of 1966? Could anyone have imagined that Communists would cease to rule Russia?

Indeed, for that matter, who would have predicted the earth-shattering changes that a hitherto obscure monk in the far reaches of the Holy Roman Empire would bring about? Who, sitting in Rome, would have predicted Martin Luther?

Martyn Lloyd-Jones believed passionately in the biblical doctrine of God's sovereignty. The same God who raised up Martin Luther tore down the Berlin Wall. God is sovereign—he can do anything. He can change the face of Evangelicalism. He can transform dead churches into life, and tear down barriers not just between countries but between his own people. The appeal of 1966 was made out of the deepest longing and desire of God's faithful servant Martyn Lloyd-Jones to see God's gospel people come together. No one can ever dissent from that. He wanted God to have all the glory, and to that all Christian people can only cry, 'Amen!' But when it comes to the methodology he chose and to his emphasis on structure rather than doctrine—of trying to speed up the pace of change rather than let events take their course and develop their own momentum—one can only echo the words of his great hero Oliver Cromwell to the Scots: 'Brother, I beseech ye in the bowels of Christ, consider whether ye be mistaken.'

The one thing the Doctor longed to see above all else was revival. To him, only if the church was purified could revival come. But surely it is revival that purifies the church? But in wanting to see a great outpouring of the Holy Spirit of God, who can blame him for his impatience? Whatever went wrong after his great appeal, no one could ever have had better motives and a greater desire to seek the heart of God than Martyn Lloyd-Jones did. For that one's only response can be to praise God for that faithfulness, and to pray that the revival for which the Doctor longed so deeply, yet never witnessed, will soon come.

9

The Latter Years
1968–1981

Retirement from the Chapel

In 1968 the Doctor became seriously ill from cancer. He had now been at Westminster Chapel for thirty years, twenty-five of them as sole pastor. His illness was very distressing for the family. But he felt that it was the Lord telling him to go on to a wider ministry, one that he could not fulfil were he to be restricted through the regular ministry at the Chapel, which involved preaching three major sermons a week. So he took the opportunity to retire, although this was emphatically retirement from the Chapel only, and not from work generally. Far from it!

Much of what the Doctor did in the last years of his life has been mentioned elsewhere, in the more thematic chapters. As we shall see from the final chapter, the last thirteen years of his life were those in which many of his family got to know him the best. This was especially true of his grandchildren. Ann's three children, Elizabeth, Rhiannon and Adam, were born after his retirement and lived in the same house as their grandparents. The young family lived on the upper floor, and it was a great joy to their grandparents to have them popping in and out to chat or to watch TV.

The extended family

In the final chapter we will be looking at the Doctor as Grandfather. However, he also had a much wider family, with whom he was able to spend more time after his retirement. First, there was his brother Sir Vincent Lloyd-Jones, the High Court Judge, with wife Ena and two children, David and Jan. Bethan Lloyd-Jones had two brothers. One was Ieaun Phillips, the Superintendent of the Forward Movement of Wales and later Moderator of the Presbyterian Church of Wales, the denomination in which the Doctor had been active in Aberavon. He and his wife Lynn had a daughter, Betsan, married to Graham Melville-Thomas, a child psychiatrist, and they in turn had three children, Rachel, Sarah and Jonathan.

Jonathan remembers his great-uncle most warmly. When the Doctor came to Cardiff, he remembers that everyone made a great fuss. This puzzled him as a child. This kind old man was his 'Uncle Martyn', to whom the whole family was devoted! As Jonathan has put it: 'People would come up to me and say, "I didn't know that your uncle was *the* Dr Martyn Lloyd-Jones." This of course came as a big surprise to me, not knowing how well-respected he was.' Children remember funny things. Young Jonathan recalls that when the Doctor came to Wales to see his relatives, 'Uncle Martyn would keep his overcoat on for long periods of time.'

Jonathan also has memories of coming up to see his uncle Martyn in Balsham. There was some adventure programme on the television, and his mother said to him, 'You're not watching this—Uncle Martyn's in the room.' However, as Jonathan has written, 'I remember Uncle Martyn saying, "No, I'll watch it—it sounds good." As a kid, I was delighted that such a man was interested in something I was interested in.' This was the

Doctor all over—if it mattered to a young great-nephew, it mattered to him.

Ieaun Phillips was the man whom he always described as very close to him; something he had been since their boyhood back at the Welsh chapel in Charing Cross Road in the early days before the First World War. They were more than just brothers-in-law. As a result, when Ieaun died in 1969 the blow was a grievous one. Interestingly, the deep warmth between the two men was despite their differing views on some fairly key subjects. One of these was the 1966 issue. Not only did Ieaun stay in his denomination, despite it being doctrinally mixed, but he was actually for some while its head!

Betsan Melville-Thomas recalls that her father, as Superintendent, would get women, known as Sisters of the People, to speak in some of the mission halls on the housing estates in Wales. As she has written, 'We knew that Uncle Martyn was opposed to women preachers, so as you can imagine the argument got quite heated. But, in spite of their differing opinions, there was no animosity between them and the friendship remained fast and firm.'

In 1969, when Ieaun Phillips died, the Doctor went down to Wales for the funeral. Betsan remembers: 'At supper that night, my mother asked Uncle Martyn to say grace at table, and he began in Welsh the old familiar family grace. After the first line his voice faltered and he said, "I have lost my best friend."

Another family group whom he greatly enjoyed seeing during these years were Bethan's cousin Nelian and her family of three girls—the second of whom was also called Bethan. Nelian Jones was more like a sister to Bethan Lloyd-Jones than a cousin, and as with the Melville-Thomas family, the relationship was always very close.

Bethan Jervois has many very fond memories of Uncle Martyn—indeed on one occasion he actually saved her

life. They feared that Bethan was 'apparently mortally ill
. . . and he came to the rescue' through a brilliant piece of
medical diagnosis. Not surprisingly, he was deeply loved
by his in-laws. As Bethan has put it, as a young man, the
Doctor had 'the common sense and wit and wisdom to
marry the beautiful Bethan Phillips'! Not only were the
Doctor and Mrs Lloyd-Jones an outstanding couple, but
they possessed 'more talent in understanding and loving
their fellow men' than most people ever could. All that
'on top of their Christian faith and teaching made them',
in their cousin's view, 'very, very special and probably
unique'.

As Bethan has put it—and this applies equally to his
grandchildren's view of him—he was simply 'always
there'. She could 'talk to him about *anything*', and for
someone in their twenties, this was vitally important, as I
too discovered. 'Any problem I had,' Bethan remembers,
'whether medical or spiritual, I knew I could always call
the Ealing number. . . . One always expected so much of
him, and he never let one down.' As we have seen, the
phone was often busy in the Lloyd-Jones household! But
as Bethan remembers from her visits there to see her older
cousins, 'he never complained when that happened, and
had all the time in the world for whoever was on the other
end'.

The wider ministry

Many of the things he had done before continued—his
involvement with IFES, the Westminster Fellowship, and
his ongoing concern both about the state of the church
and of the need for revival. But there were some new
emphases.

Although the Doctor took some time to recuperate
fully from surgery, he was not idle for long. The faculty

at Westminster Theological Seminary in Philadelphia, USA, asked him to give a series of lectures on the nature of preaching. This he agreed to do, and the result which was subsequently published as *Preaching and Preachers* became a classic. It was in these lectures that he described preaching as 'logic on fire', perhaps the best description ever given of biblical exposition.

However, now that he was not under pressure to produce three new sermons weekly, he could concentrate on the systematic publication of some of his major series at Westminster Chapel.

This meant that we saw far more of him in the family than before. If he was in Ealing, where he retained his London home, he was permanently in demand, usually on the telephone. However much he might have retired from the Chapel, he was now more active than ever as the Chairman of the Westminster Fellowship. The pastoral needs of those who had followed him out of their denominations in 1966 were often considerable and involved him in giving the pastor in question a great deal of his time. He also had visitors, not just from Britain but from all over the world. (This was always a slight strain on Bethan who, while enjoying visitors, always wanted the house to be immaculately tidy before any of them came!)

Consequently, therefore, if he were to do any serious work on the manuscripts—all his sermons at the Chapel had been carefully transcribed since the war—he needed much peace and quiet, along with people who would screen his phone calls. This meant that the best place to carry out the work was at our home in Balsham, far away from the bustle of London life. (The telephone entry in Ealing was under B. Lloyd-Jones—for Bethan—for the same reason, but those who knew this could always get in touch with him there.) He would bring his battered old brown briefcase and his transcripts, and set to work. As he did so, it was interesting to see how sometimes the truth as it came through his own sermons had the power to move him deeply; this was especially so, for instance, when he came to the final verses of Ephesians 3.

The main series brought out in his lifetime were those on Romans and Ephesians. Characteristically, he did not bring them out in chronological order, but in order of importance! Nowadays people buying the set do so in biblical sequence, but he felt that pastorally, some ought to come out before others, and his publisher agreed. Some of these volumes were edited in his lifetime and published in Britain by the Banner of Truth (the one that came out with the Evangelical Press was later taken over by the Banner) and contained his very clear teaching on the sealing of the Holy Spirit. As we have seen, we were somewhat surprised when considerable discussion broke out over his views on the work of the Holy Spirit in *Joy Unspeakable*, since he said nothing in that which he had not said before in the Banner volumes. A favourite was, and is, *Life in the Spirit* in the Ephesians series. It showed, among other things, his teaching on how to bring up and encourage children; something that we much appreciated from him in day-to-day life.

His books sold worldwide. I never forgot receiving a letter from someone in a remote area of Borneo, thanking me for one of them. On another occasion, I was at a meeting in Florida where a complete stranger came up to me and asked: 'Are you the grandson of Dr D. Martyn Lloyd-Jones?' On hearing that I was, he asked me to sign his Bible forthwith, not through any merit of my own, but because he so admired the Doctor's writing! In my career I have been inside many a pastor's room, and it is always gratifying to see a large set of the Doctor's books. My parents even saw his books in the chaplain's study in West Point Military Academy!

Another of the Doctor's main activities in retirement was to speak in the churches of men who had come out of their denominations in 1966, or who were in small, struggling 'causes' and needed his encouragement. He felt very close to such men, some of whom had suffered greatly for their adherence to his views. Needless to say, in such places, the excitement when the Doctor came was tremendous! The great man himself—*here*. Sometimes he would just attend a small church on a Sunday. I remember being with him on one occasion, and the young pastor, alarmed to see the Doctor in a back pew, suddenly announced he was changing his sermon to something else! (While this man would never have imitated the Doctor, there were those whose imitation of him was very strong, and there were times when he almost heard one of his own sermons!)

In 1980 he became too ill to go on preaching. His last service, fittingly, was in Barcombe, in a little Baptist chapel, whose pastor Ray Gaydon we saw earlier as a member of Westminster Chapel. He became very frail from the cancer and found walking painful. Thankfully his mind was active to the last, although at the very end his voice left him. He had to scribble notes to us, so that we could know what he was thinking. He obviously knew that his end was in sight. He cancelled his newspaper in advance, to stop on the 28th February. One of his last messages to the family was, 'Don't pray for healing. Don't try to hold me back from the glory.'[85] He died on the 1st March 1981, in his sleep. It was a doubly symbolic day— St David's Day, the national day of his beloved Wales, and that year it was also a Sunday, the Lord's day.

Jim Packer has written:

For me, those last words, 'the glory', point with precision to the significance that under God he had in my life. He embodied and expressed 'the glory'—the glory of God, of Christ, of grace, of the gospel, of the Christian ministry, of humanness according to the new creation—more richly than any man I have ever known. No man can give another a greater gift than a vision of such glory as this. I am forever in his debt.[86]

That moving tribute captures what his family felt about the Doctor as well. He was now able to enjoy what he described to the congregation in Aberavon on the 50th Anniversary Service in 1977, when he came back to see his old friends. He preached a wonderful sermon on 1 Corinthians 2:2, 'For I determined not to know anything among you, save Jesus Christ, and him crucified.'[87] It was the first sermon he ever preached at Aberavon, and now he preached it again. After a stirring gospel address, he concluded about the work of Christ: 'He will regenerate you and you will become a saint, and you will follow after that glorious company of saints that have left this very place and are now basking in the sunshine of his face in the glory everlasting.'[88]

On his gravestone in Wales are the very words of his text: 'For I determined not to know any thing among you, save Jesus Christ, and him crucified.' That message was at the heart of the Doctor's life, and was all that he stood for. He gave us all a powerful sense of the presence and glory of God, and he is now with God. Now Martyn Lloyd-Jones is 'basking in the sunshine of his face in the glory everlasting'.[89]

Hallelujah! Praise God for the life of such a faithful servant as Martyn Lloyd-Jones.

10

Grandfather

To his six grandchildren he was 'Dadcu' or, in our affections, simply the world's best grandfather possible. Actually, he was in reality 'Dacu' (*pron.* Da-kee) since as a small child I never learned to spell the Welsh word properly, and so to me, for twenty-six years of my life, he was Dacu, and that is how I thought of him then and have done so since. In fact even to have called him 'Dadcu' was strictly speaking wrong, as it was the diminutive, when translated into English, of 'beloved father', which to us he was not. But be that as it may, he was certainly our most beloved grandfather.

He had six grandchildren altogether, rather neatly arranged in three of each sex—three grandsons and three grand-daughters. The first three were Catherwoods—Christopher (Martyn) (1955), Bethan (1958) and Jonathan (1961), followed by the three Desmonds—Elizabeth (1968), Rhiannon (1970) and Adam (Martyn) (1971), making a sixteen-year gap between the eldest and youngest. In some ways we all knew him equally well—the Catherwoods because we were older and the Desmonds because they lived in the same house, living upstairs from their grandparents.

Suffice it to say that his help to his grandchildren in moments of great need and personal urgency was immense. He knew, for example, the pressures that

171

they must have gone through simply by being his grand-children, and the often ludicrously unfair expectations that people had of them. One of his deepest held con-victions, which can be seen in his chapters on parent-hood in his classic and much-loved work *Life in the Spirit*, is that everyone is an individual. Now that should go without saying. But the 'PKs' (preacher's kids), as clergy families are known in the States and increasingly in Britain as well, are often under immense pressure. The father, or in our case the grandfather, may have been called to the ministry, but that does not mean the children are as well.

His chapter in the book, 'Balanced Discipline', is surely one of the greatest expositions on the Apostle Paul's injunction to fathers in Ephesians, 'Provoke not your children unto wrath,' or, as he and later the NIV rendered it, 'Do not exasperate your children!' He knew, for example, at Westminster Chapel, that an espe-cially close eye was often kept on his grandchildren, who were, of course, expected to be models of perfect beha-viour at all times! To one of them, this turned out to be an especial burden, as youthful exuberance was often more in keeping with that child's style than a sober, quiet attitude to what, for children, was an unusually long Sunday. (As we have seen, Sunday at the Chapel could be very long—from 11am through to at least 5pm for those who did not stay to the evening service.) At least his poor grandchild did have a very strong sense of humour—one very much inherited from the Doctor. The two stern members of the Chapel who gave the poor grandchild such a hard time were named, purely by chance, but much to the family's amusement, Mr Gilbert and Mr Sullivan. . . .

At one stage, Jonathan, his middle grandson, was particularly influenced by Eastern mysticism, with some of the lifestyle consequences that went with it. Jonathan had been strongly influenced in particular by a Tibetan mystic, who had gone into print.

Now the Doctor was very concerned for two reasons. First, and obviously, because of the enormous affection he had for Jonathan. They had a mutually shared interest, in which they spent many happy hours together, and which gave them a close bond. Consequently they spent much time talking together and the Doctor was very aware of how Jonathan felt about things. Secondly he was concerned because of the spiritual tragedy he saw: that of someone being so led astray and deceived by the evil one.

But consistent with his own teaching, he did not come down in a heavy-handed way and forbid Jonathan ever to read such material, as many Christian parents would have felt it their duty to do. Far from it! Rather, he asked himself, what was it about the teachings of this Buddhist that so attracted Jonathan?

For he had one very important guiding principle which is best summed up in the well-known yet very true catchphrase, apposite above all in this case: 'God has no grandchildren.' It was that we all come to Christ as individuals. Who our parents are makes no difference. Look at his own family. He was an evangelical leader, his brother Vincent an Anglo-Catholic, yet both of them had had exactly the same upbringing. No, everyone had to become a Christian for themselves, and the fact that children were raised in a godly Christian home made no ultimate difference. It was always something individual, between that person as a unique creation of God and their Maker. The fact that Jonathan was his grandchild was of no consequence here.

So he decided that the best thing to do was to read the book that had been so influential. As it happened, the book had an unusually garish cover displaying an oriental face with the Tibetan tantric third eye in the middle of the

forehead! One day, after giving a sermon somewhere, the
Doctor settled down to read the book on his way back to
London. As he told the family afterwards, he sat there
wondering what on earth other people in the compart-
ment were making of someone they might just have heard
preaching reading a book so bizarre! But despite any
embarrassment this might have caused, he read it all the
same, because it mattered to one of his grandchildren and
therefore was of great importance to him.

As his daughter Elizabeth has said, he 'read it with
care. He read it seriously. He took notes on it, and
when he came back he went through it with' Jonathan.
Indeed, while some had a tendency with young ones to
say, 'For goodness sake, that's all rubbish,' the Doctor did
nothing of the kind. Elizabeth has commented: 'He
wanted to know just what it was that was getting hold
of his grandchild.' He said what points were good, and
pointed out where they were dangerous. And because he
had read it, he knew the book far better than Jonathan
did. Consequently, the information he had acquired made
him better able to deal with this kind of problem. He
cared and it showed.

He was also the kind of wise and loving grandfather
with whom one could discuss absolutely anything. He was
unshockable, creating an environment in which we felt
able to raise any subject with him. Maybe it was his
training as a doctor, where his insights into the lives of
the wealthy and well-known proved a key factor in leading
him into the ministry. Of course, being in the pastorate
itself, listening to many people's problems had the same
effect. But it was especially helpful to us as grandchildren.

Grandparents, too, have a special relationship with the
third generation, as they have the love that parents have,
but can love at one generation removed. This also helped
good relations, but even grandparents can be huffy and

shockable. Not the Doctor! Whatever the problem was—
whether Eastern mysticism, or a phone call in the early
hours of the morning on the question of the validity of the
gift of tongues—he was there to speak to us and to listen
to whatever we had to say.

One incident shows the same point in a very different
way. Aged about six, I noticed that there was a word that
grown-ups sometimes referred to and boys at school
sniggered at. My grandfather and I were sitting next to
each other, both reading and having lunch together.
Suddenly, knowing that there was nothing I could not
ask Dacu, I turned to him and asked, 'Dacu, what do
you think about sex?'

In retrospect, it must have been difficult for him not to
laugh. But his response revealed another side of him that
applied not only to his own grandchildren but indeed to
all the children he met. He always believed in taking
children at their own valuation. If it was comic to an
adult—an earnest six-year-old asking naively about this
mysterious thing called sex—to the child it was a perfectly serious question. He told me that God created sex
and made it proper within marriage like Mummy and
Daddy had, but that it was really a question to ask
when I was older.

A Christian leader now eminent in the evangelical
world once told me of how his parents nearly scared
him to death about a visit by the Doctor to their home.
My grandfather's eminence, while meaning a lot to the
parents, who were rather awestruck that he was visiting
their home, meant nothing to the child. So when the great
man came to their home, they were amazed to discover
how kind he was to the young son of the house. To the
Doctor, who always hated flummery and being given
special treatment, it was probably a relief that someone
in the house was not treating him with awe—at least to

one person he was just an ordinary human being. But the Doctor was always natural with children, and for his six grandchildren, the children who saw him the most, this was an enormous bonus. We certainly had no reason to fear a visit by our grandfather.

Another example, which I have been asked to put in this book, shows his great wisdom. One of his grandchildren, Bethan, was a big fan of a well-known footballer. Now there was nothing wrong in this per se of course, nor was the enthusiasm discouraged by anyone. But a problem arose none the less.

This was because the footballer in question was coming to London—on a Sunday. Needless to say, this sparked off a lot of family debate. What was more important—a footballer or Sunday school? Some members of the family had no doubts—and it was not the footballer!

However, rather to the family's general astonishment, the Doctor was in favour of letting young Bethan go to see the footballer instead. So to Bethan's great joy off went one parent and a happy child. She would grow up, the Doctor argued, and would come in her own time to spiritual things in the Lord's providence. It was also wrong to be rigid on Sunday observance with someone who was not yet a Christian. While Sunday school was important, exceptions should be permissible.

Maybe this story also illustrates the fact that the Doctor practised the gifts of the Spirit. But regardless of that, when Bethan turned up that Sunday afternoon, things were not as they, or indeed anyone else, had expected. It was, contrary to hopes, a rather dreary day. But to crown it all, the footballer decided not to turn up because of the weather, so everyone who was there had waited in vain! How right the Doctor was. Instead of Bethan's desire to visit the footballer being forbidden fruit, she had had a lesson in the ways of the world.

Not long after, she was able to touch the footballer's sweaty shirt! (Not with him present, I should add.) And she eventually became a Christian herself, as her wise grandfather had prayed she would.

Whether the Doctor had had some word from the Lord, or whether it was the spiritual common sense of a man whose life was dedicated to the Lord's service, he did not tell us. But it showed how he put into practice with his own grandchildren the things he preached from the pulpit of Westminster Chapel. His theology was consistent with his life—and for that, although we did not know the causes at the time, we were profoundly thankful.

In my own spiritual walk, his influence was total, even though as the years progressed we did not agree on everything. In 1966, when I was eleven years old, I remember hearing a sermon of his taken from the book of Acts. At the time it was more a treat to go and hear 'Dacu preach the evening service' than anything else. Westminster Chapel was one of those churches where provision was really only made for the very young not to be in the service. Sunday school was in the afternoon.

Fortunately, my parents did not expect us to listen to the sermons, reckoning accurately that when you are little, you are not really equipped to listen to sermons on the theology of the Holy Spirit! So it was not for another twenty years that I ever discovered, when editing *Joy Unspeakable* and *Prove All Things* as a publisher, what momentous material my grandfather had been preaching. So during the morning service, we were able to draw. I invented all kinds of imaginary worlds and characters, some of whom I introduced to my grandfather, who, on one occasion, spent some time giving me advice about the rulers of the world I had created and who was suitable for which post!

However, once we were old enough to go to the evening

service, we were expected, as was proper, to listen. I remember a sermon in which my grandfather was critical of a state visit being made to some country or other by the then Pope, his point being that to combine a spiritual office with that of a head of state was quite wrong.

But it was the sermon from Acts which changed my young life. His evening sermons, as we have seen, were primarily evangelistic, though of course he expected Christians to gain from and benefit by them as well. Suddenly his words grabbed my attention. He spoke of a lady in another church who played a prominent role in that congregation's life. When she heard that he preached mainly in the morning for Christians and for non-Christians at night, the Holy Spirit had clearly convicted her, as she realised her own spiritual condition. Eminent in the life of that church she may have been, but she was not truly born again and she needed to be so.

I realised that I was in the same state as that lady. I had never been a rebel, and never been particularly conscious of sin, yet despite my own quite extraordinary Christian heritage, of which as an eleven-year-old boy I was only dimly aware, I needed to be a Christian too.

Years later, I cannot recall whether it was then and there that I became a Christian or whether that sermon started a process at the end of which I was born again. On a family holiday when I was twelve I remember thinking that I had now been a Christian for a year, so it must have been some time around that sermon that I was converted.

Of course, to us, our grandfather was Dacu, but somehow, when he put on that black Geneva gown that was his hallmark, he ceased to be my grandfather and became not so much 'the Doctor', because being his grandchild I could never see him as others did, but none the less the messenger of God faithfully proclaiming the Scriptures to someone such as me, who needed to hear it just as much as anyone else did. So although God has no grand-children, and although everyone comes to faith in Jesus Christ as Saviour and Lord not through their parents or grandparents but through their own conversion through Christ on the cross, I had, none the less, in God's provi-dence, become a Christian, humanly speaking, through a sermon of my own grandfather's. In fact this was ironic, as he had resisted attempts to talk to me about coming to faith earlier, perhaps because he sensed that the Lord was at work and could be trusted with my eternal salvation.

Because coming from a very Christian family can be a hindrance to true conversion, my parents had wisely never put any pressure on any of us children to become Christians—though there must surely have been times, as with all parents, when they would have dearly loved to! As we have seen, the Doctor was also very sensitive to this, helped by this strong and abiding belief in the sovereignty of God.

So one could say that up to my conversion, albeit at the young age of eleven, my background was paradoxically not a help to my Christian life, especially as I was an easy-going kind of child, although it certainly put me, as they say, 'under the sound of the gospel'. One only has to read the biographies of great Christians of the past to see that a godly home is no guarantee of true conversion, with descendants of illustrious heroes of the faith lapsing either into dead formalism or into outright, if not actually bitter, rejection of the parental faith.

However, once I had been converted, the privilege of my background was incalculable: indeed, I never fully appre-ciated it until after my grandfather's death in 1981. Much of this privilege stemmed from the relaxed, highly acces-sible and close-knit relationship the Doctor had with his family. He loved us all dearly and it showed.

We were of vital importance to him, and he wanted us

all to know it. We were his flesh and blood. This meant, to him, total access. He was always there when we needed him, and however small our need might seem to others, it was important to him because of the relationship we had with him. Much of what people have written about the Doctor shows that he was, objectively speaking, a rather shy man. Certainly he was not one for small talk. He hated chit-chat and social fripperies, and always felt deeply uneasy in such environments. Give him a meaty theological argument any time! But, of course, this could make him deeply intimidating to the unwary.

Someone who subsequently got to know him well, Gaius Davies, has described something of this in his chapter on him called 'The Doctor as a Doctor'. He was a Welshman, like Dr Lloyd-Jones, and was a student at Bart's in the 1940s, therefore you would have expected him to have addressed the Doctor with great ease. But of his weekly visits to the Friday night discussions at Westminster Chapel he writes:

> The views of members of the audience were sought by Dr Lloyd-Jones as chairman, and then discussed as fully as possible, showing with wit and humour where such views logically led. I remember being full of admiration for those who spoke up: one voice I recall above others was that of Fred Catherwood, later to be well-known! I feel ashamed as I look back, at my silence; I was as mixed up in my thinking as any and should have been one of those publicly helped to be sorted out. When Mrs. Lloyd-Jones once asked me why I did not speak up on Friday nights, my reply was that I considered it unwise to stand in the path of a steam-roller. But the Doctor was a very gentle steam-roller, and he was particularly kind to the young and weak in the faith.[90]

A gentle steam roller! Well, his grandchildren certainly never thought of him like that. But sadly others did. He

once put it to me, 'People are accustomed to being silent
in my presence.' So unlike his grandson!

Maybe it was his shyness in social intercourse, but there
was also a formality about him. Now some of this was, as
we have seen, the same propensity to wear jacket, tie,
waistcoat and hat on the beach, not to mention socks
and black shoes! But John Stott, who also knew him
well over many years, has written of him: 'Dr. Lloyd-
Jones could give an impression of sternness in the pulpit
and of shyness in his correspondence. Even letters to his
friends began "My dear Sir", and he would seldom sign
himself by his Christian name. Yet, when counselling
individuals in his vestry or study, he could not have
been more sympathetic and affectionate.'[91]

While kindness personified, he was shy, and it was
really only with family and a very few select friends that
he was truly relaxed. This is why his family, including his
grandchildren, were so important to him. With us he
could be completely at ease.

He was a marvellous listener. This was one of the most
wonderful things to us as his grandchildren. He was not
just busy, but far busier than most. Visiting his home, not
only would he often be preparing sermons or a talk, but,
or so it seemed to us, half the world would be ringing him
up! He took his duties as 'pastor's pastor' very seriously
indeed, especially those ministers who were members of
the fraternal that met under his aegis at the Chapel, and
this was often over 200 people. Many of them had problems or queries that had to be answered over the phone,
and this he often did. But when we arrived, business was
despatched and full attention was given to whatever we
had to say. Furthermore, he really listened, as we could
tell from the questions he would ask back. This made a
huge difference, and the complaint that children so often

make, that older people do not really listen, was never so
with him.

Indeed, we did not realise at the time what a privilege
this was. By definition, the ministers in his circle saw him
face to face maybe once a month at most, and then
usually in the company of many others. For them a phone
call was the one time they had with him direct. Whereas
we saw him all the time—either when he was in London
quite frequently, or when he came to Balsham, the
Catherwood country home near Cambridge. In fact this
was a further privilege, since only a few could ever ring
him there—one of the reasons for staying with us was so
that he could edit his sermons in peace. But these times
were for us usually during school or university holiday, so
we were always there when he was. We therefore had
access to him at a time when no one else did. Once
again, we only really understood quite how special this
was when he was no longer there.

Paradoxically, this meant that in his lifetime I seldom
read any of his books; something ironic in that much of
my life since his death has been the task of editing his
manuscripts for publication. For many people, his books
were the only way of knowing what he thought, of gaining
his unique expertise into what the Scriptures were telling
us. But for me, if I wanted to know what he thought, I had
only to ask him!

When he was with us at Balsham, he would often initiate
the discussion himself. He was, when with us there,
usually editing his sermons. He had a favourite, slightly
battered old chair in our small sitting room, inhabited
quite often just by him and his grandchildren—we knew
to be silent when Dacu was there. (When visitors came, he
would go to his familiar place on the green sofa in the
bigger sitting room next door.) The room was called 'The
Morning Room', and while it was true that he was often

there in the mornings, it is also correct to say that he was often there past midnight! Rather than use a desk, he would take an even more battered old briefcase, put his sermon transcripts on the case and start to work, his pencil in hand! (I have edited many of his posthumous books sitting in exactly the same chair, surrounded by his bookshelves from his London home, which used to be in a special room at the back of his bedroom.)

As a result, the passage he had just been editing was often at the forefront of his mind. This would therefore form part of meal-time discussion. So although I did not always read what he said, I was familiar with it.

His son-in-law has described those meal times:

> While I always regarded his views with the greatest respect, not so his grandchildren. To them he was only 'Dadcu' . . . and whatever views he held were there to be disputed, together with the views of the rest of their elders. He was like an old lion with young cubs which darted in and out where no one else would dare to go, while he tolerated from them what he would tolerate from no one else.
>
> And within the family debate, where he did not have to worry about misrepresentation, he would set them off with the most outrageous statements, and as they came spluttering back, 'You can't possibly say that,' he would defend them with all his forensic skill.
>
> We used to have tremendous discussions in the family about politics. Although he had, throughout his public life, attacked the idea of a social gospel and, as a kind of overrun from that, tended to the view that there was no Christian attitude to politics, he was nevertheless fascinated by the whole political process. He used to watch political debate on television with enormous zest, and report to us on programmes we had missed.[92]

Politics was an interest that he and I both shared. With us it came across in two ways. I was fascinated by history, taking an A-level and then, like his younger daughter Ann, going on to read history at Oxford. (It was in fact he who told me that I had gained a place at Balliol—the college rang my parents' home in London to say that I had been successful, but the family had already left for Balsham. However, the Doctor just happened to be there on his way up to join us, and so was there to answer the call. He thereupon bought me a present—a biography of Lady Jane Grey, the strongly Puritan 'Nine Days Queen', written by the Catholic historian David Mathew. It was an interesting choice of present which indicated the width of his own reading.)

Many have written of the Doctor's own love of history, and one can see it everywhere, not just in the specifically historical lectures that he gave on the Puritans and other subjects, but even in his evangelistic sermons, where the lessons of history proved the futility of man without God.

My own interest was, and has remained, the history of the 1920s and 1930s. While as we have seen the Doctor rejected the social gospel, the historian in him never ceased to be fascinated by the period, especially as it was one that he knew well. So he was more than pleased to have a member of the family who shared his love of that time—something he and I shared with his brother Vincent, who had kept up his own direct involvement in Liberal politics while at the Bar, and who had been active at the time.

Needless to say, whenever a book on Lloyd-George or Churchill came out, my grandfather devoured the reviews and made sure to tell me! Quite often, the book would appear as a birthday or Christmas present. Other times he would buy a book for himself and then pass it on to me. I possess all the original set of the official biography of Winston Churchill, not just the later volumes by Martin Gilbert, but the early volumes by Randolph Churchill too.

These were a gift from my grandfather, and when I look now in second-hand bookshops at how much a complete set of the standard edition now sells for, I am even more grateful for his gift! It is worth adding that while the Doctor was a passionate supporter of Churchill's stand against the dictators in the 1930s, he always maintained that Lloyd-George, the architect of victory in the First World War, was by far the greater man and that Churchill himself had said so.

One of the Doctor's most significant traits was his enormous enthusiasm. This made him tremendously supportive of whatever one did. You almost got the impression that if you achieved something, he was as excited as you were! This was of course in proportion to the age of the person—he was as excited with the school achievements of his younger grandchildren as he was by the success of his older grandchildren at university. This was a massive boost to the morale, especially at an age when it is all too easy to become discouraged. Nothing was too good for us!

Our other political discussions were of a more theological nature. As we have seen, he opposed the idea of politics being able to bring about change. So far as that went, I agreed with him. But at the time, I considered politics as an option, with thoughts of entering that field. (My later life has proved him right—like him I entered full-time Christian work, albeit of a different kind, while retaining an outsider's interest in the whole political process.)

I was very influenced by the interpretation of Francis Schaeffer, some of whose family I knew, and whose books made a great impact on me, as indeed they did on many of my student generation. In particular, Schaeffer's idea of Christ being the Lord of the whole of reality appealed to me greatly. The London L'Abri was then in Ealing, and I often went there, as did my sister Bethan.

To my grandfather, this cultural mandate theology, as he would put it, simply did not work. Our duty was to proclaim the gospel, because it was only regeneration that could change things. He did of course hold Schaeffer in high esteem personally, while not agreeing with all his views. He had a funny story about the Schaeffers that may have slightly coloured his own reactions, albeit in a very benign way.

Back in the 1950s he journeyed to L'Abri with his wife Bethan. Schaeffer and the Doctor had known each other since the 1940s, when Schaeffer had visited England shortly after his call to come and live in Europe. On this occasion, however, the Doctor was coming over to Switzerland to conduct the wedding service of the eldest Schaeffer daughter, Priscilla. It was a long journey, and the two Lloyd-Joneses arrived late at night and utterly exhausted—which for a natural owl like the Doctor was unusual.

However, on their arrival, they were warmly greeted by Francis Schaeffer, who immediately wished to get down to the business of serious discussion. Almost the first thing he asked his guest was, 'Tell me, Dr Lloyd-Jones, what is truth?' This became something of a byword in our family, and if one of us wanted to discuss some great theological or similar topic late at night, long after others were falling asleep, the phrase, 'What is truth?' would appear to curtail all further discussion!

But when it came to the views of his Schaefferite grandson, I think that what mattered more to him was not that he and I disagreed, but that I had a thought-through position which to me expressed what the biblical truth was on a given matter. So far as the family were concerned, agreement with his views was never a prerequisite of love and devotion. He loved us unconditionally. We were his own. I'm sure he would have loved us all the same even if we were passionate Arminians! At least my views of Schaeffer's theology were within the Reformed spectrum, as was Schaeffer himself.

Sadly, as Jim Packer's writings have shown, the Doctor's views on ecclesiology led to a parting of the ways and to a severing of old friendships. This particular severance caused much sorrow in the family, as some of us held Packer in the very highest regard. My mother had been friends with him ever since her student days and her father's separation with Dr Packer made no difference to her friendship with him and Kit Packer. I had of course been greatly influenced by his works, especially *Knowing God*, and when a student by his speaking as well. Fortunately Dr Packer bore no ill will towards any of us about his lost friendship, which was a great relief. Many years later he was to write that the Doctor was the greatest man he ever knew.

Within the family, though, disagreement on this subject was perfectly permissible, deeply though the Doctor held to his views. The fact is that his own family was by no means united on it. We could of course see exactly what he meant, and that there was a strong case for secession. Maybe it was even right to secede. But, once again, perhaps Schaeffer was right—secede yourself, but do not make this the basis for fellowship. Much of this has been discussed in Chapter 8, so we can look at it here in the family context.

Our grandmother Bethan was the model of the very loyal wife, and in her own lifetime she never made known in public her very private views. Sadly, it is really only now that she is no longer with us that one can allude to them here. She was in an awkward spot because her own very beloved brother Ieuan Phillips had been the Moderator of a 'mixed denomination'. Although he died not long after 1966, he never seceded, and when he died his brother-in-law, the Doctor, was to say that he had lost his closest friend. Likewise a cousin of my grandmother's, albeit not a relative to whom she was close, was Glyn Simon. Here the situation was worse—he was no less than the Archbishop of Wales! (I am afraid that as children we loved to tease our Gu with, 'Your cousin the Archbishop . . . !')

Both the Doctor's daughters had attended an Anglican church when students at Oxford, in both cases before 1966 of course. However, when I went up in 1973, an obvious problem arose. The Doctor's successor as minister of Westminster Chapel, J. Glyn Owen, was friends with Keith Weston, a wonderful, warm and very godly man who had a church in Oxford. So why not go there? Well, the church was Anglican—St Ebbe's (in fact the same church my mother and aunt had attended, but under different rectors). There was of course discussion!

But when I went up to Oxford, I went to St Ebbe's with his full knowledge and permission. While there were Free Churches in Oxford, there was little doubt at the time that the active spiritual life was in a church like St Ebbe's. For me, spiritually and pastorally, it was very much the right decision. Keith Weston knew of course about my background. But I was still very much an individual in my own right, with my own needs. The Doctor sensed this, and so never objected. It was never an issue between us.

He visited me several times in Oxford; visits I will always treasure, especially as one of them had a revolutionary effect on my prayer life (which I regret I have not been able to keep up consistently since). It was that prayer should always begin with praise, not a shopping list. Of course we know this from the Lord's Prayer, but how often we forget it.

He spoke at the OICCU (the Christian Union). Many

of the students from Anglican homes were amazed that he was still alive—they thought that like Spurgeon he was one of the great giants of the nineteenth century! (This to me was a sad reflection on the extent to which his influence in wider evangelical circles had declined.)

The Doctor was well-known to the OICCU President, Lindsay Brown, an able student and fellow Welshman. Through Lindsay, another Welsh student at Oxford, Gareth Lewis, got to know Dr Lloyd-Jones. At a conference some years after, Gareth spotted me asleep, with a book by a well-regarded Anglican Evangelical on my lap. He instantly photographed me and sent the photo to the Doctor, who loved it!

Characteristically, one of the Doctor's visits to me in Oxford was not without controversy. We were about to have a big OICCU mission to the university, with the late David Watson as missioner. The Doctor, as we have seen, was rather chary of organised missions, and said so in an interview he gave a Christian student newspaper. So soon before the mission, this created a major stir! As it turned out, in the providence of God, the mission was an outstanding success, with many lasting, genuine conversions. But the Doctor's point was well made—if Christians did their duty properly and shared the gospel on a regular basis, then missions should be unnecessary. As always, his views challenged us all to think, even though we did not always agree with them.

One point of his visits to Oxford always made me laugh. As mentioned earlier, the Free Churches were at the time not as strong as the Anglicans, especially as churches such as St Ebbe's or St Aldate's were within easy walking distance for most students. (Lindsay, energetic even then, was an exception, walking some distance to a church attended by one of the Doctor's friends, the late S. M. Houghton.) Some way out, by student standards, there was a church with a godly but elderly minister, for whom the Doctor used to preach every year.

Of course, all those of us from Free Church backgrounds who, like me, were term-time Anglicans, went that once a year to hear my grandfather preach, as did, I think, some students who were Anglican by conviction. The result was that when he went there, my grandfather saw a packed congregation full of students! We all had to persuade him that this was not the norm, which in fact he understood. But it always made him wish that one day there would be in Oxford the kind of city-centre, powerful, expository and Free Church student ministry that existed in 'the other place', in Cambridge.

When his second grandchild and eldest grand-daughter Bethan went to university, things were different. She went to Nottingham. There was an outstanding Free Church there, led by Peter Lewis, one of the Doctor's more brilliant young followers; someone who had heeded his 1966 call to come out of a mixed denomination, and who was very much in tune with the Doctor's thinking on the baptism with the Holy Spirit. Not only that, but Peter was a Welshman too! Furthermore, for Bethan, the choice was as inspired for her as St Ebbe's had proved for me. She was seen very much as a person in her own right, and although she now lives in London she has maintained close links with the church, and with Peter and Valerie Lewis, ever since.

One of the most special times for us as grandchildren was Christmas. This is quite normal of course, but for us, the added factor was that he was there as well.

We always spent this at Balsham, often after having a dinner with the other members of the family in Ealing— the Desmonds in turn would come up to Balsham for the New Year.

Our Cambridgeshire home—Sutton Hall—was a

rambling old rectory when my parents first saw it, but had, in its foundations, once been the property of an Elizabethan, Sir Thomas Sutton (hence the name). It was an ideal bolt-hole from the busy world, and for younger children, as we were when we first moved there, it was paradise itself, as the grounds were a wonderful place to explore and play games of 'let's pretend'. (This was even more the case when we first moved in, as it was a bit of a jungle. In playing a game of rescuing the princess, I found a fifteenth-century ruined wall in the thicket that we had not realised was there! It is now a place equally loved by the Doctor's young great-grandchildren.)

Both Dr and Mrs Lloyd-Jones loved it too, and with characteristic generosity helped us with it. It was the perfect place for them. They desperately needed a place where they could get some peace and quiet, especially when the Doctor decided to spend most of his time turning his old sermons into books. (We have his transcripts there still, up in the attic.) Sutton Hall proved the ideal location—peaceful, but surrounded by his loving family, who could act as human buffers between him and the outside world.

So come Christmas itself, come spring and come the summer holidays, when they would stay for several weeks and sometimes look after it for us when we went abroad or to Wales or Scotland for the family holiday, the two of them would arrive.

There was always tremendous excitement when 'Gu and Dacu's car' came up the long gravel drive. My grandfather would always wear his hat to drive, even inside the car. Once, just as he was approaching our house, he forgot himself in the village and was cautioned for speeding! He had not been going very fast, of course, but it did make us laugh.

Christmas and summer were always the special holidays to me (summer because exams were over and I could relax totally—Balsham was the perfect post-exam place).

Christmas revealed the enthusiast in the Doctor, the clan patriarch—which of course he was. Christmas morning itself was unique, and for some of us, because of that, it has never really been the same since he died. There is a gap at the table which can never be filled.

We used to go to the big old dining room, much of whose furniture he and my grandmother had given us. We all sat around the table and opened our presents, and our grandfather loved to see us open ours. It fascinated him to see what each of his grandchildren had received—often we could choose our gifts, so our choices revealed a lot about us.

He was especially interested if we had books. He loved to share in our enjoyment of them. There was something special about a book—its touch, its feel. A good book was a friend, something to be with you for life, and I often pause and have a look in my own library at the books he gave me, and the books from others, that he saw me open all those years ago. Although many of his books (except the ones he gave to members of his family in his lifetime) are now in the London Theological Seminary library in London, I have, as mentioned earlier, most of the bookshelves on which he shelved them when alive. How he would have enjoyed seeing the books from all those Christmases in Balsham on his shelves!

So naturally, when we opened a present, after thanking the family member who gave them to us (if present), the second thing we did was to show them to Dacu! As we have seen, my history books interested him greatly, especially the biographies—he loved biography, as can be seen from any cursory glance at his sermons, and he instilled the same love in all of us. My sister Bethan's love of literature was one that he also shared, and her gifts were of equal fascination to him. (He left her many of his books on literature after his death, and she too has several of his shelves on which to house those and other books.)

Since I was by nature quiet and bookish he never minded if I sat next to him in the Morning Room, reading my new books as he got on with other things. Often, as the owls in the family, we would still be there, gone midnight, while all the others had gone to bed.

Christmas Day, we often had the midday meal out and the evening meal in. The Doctor, ever mindful of the cooks, wanted to give them the day off! We usually returned home in time to see the Queen's Broadcast. (Not that the Doctor was a keen royalist—he met the Queen only once, and then in spite of himself, as a favour to the Queen's physician, Dr Margery Blackie, who was an evangelical Christian and a member of Westminster Chapel for many years.)

For some years we went to a hotel in Royston, before transferring to one in Newmarket. As is clear from a reading of *Preaching and Preachers*, the Doctor believed strongly that one should never crack jokes in the pulpit. First, the idea that one needed jokes to get people's attention was something he did not believe—if one was saying something truly important and from God himself, through preaching of the Scripture, people would listen all right! But secondly, and more seriously still, is the reason he gave to Carl Henry, printed in *Christianity Today* in 1980.

Henry commented, 'You have a great sense of humour, your friends say, but seldom use it in the pulpit.' The Doctor replied, 'I find it very difficult to be humorous in the pulpit. I always feel in the pulpit that I am in the terrible position of standing between God and souls that may go to hell. That position is too appalling for humour.'

But with us, on Christmas Day, he could be seen wearing a paper hat and cracking jokes. There was in fact no contradiction. In the pulpit he was proclaiming the counsel of God to a fallen world, whereas with us he was the paterfamilias simply enjoying himself with his family. He and his brother Vincent specialised in puns, and while we groaned from time to time, they were invariably funny and always clever.

Usually there was some gentle altercation between father-in-law and son-in-law on who paid the bill, but it was always settled amicably. When he died, we stopped going out for lunch. Maybe it was convenience, or perhaps it was because the chief guest had gone. . . .

Summer holidays were quite extraordinary. Nothing with the Doctor was ever predictable, but there was a pattern to a Balsham summer that he usually followed and to which one could always look forward.

After breakfast, which was not always early, he would spend some time on his sermons. Then he would have a break for a game of croquet, followed by some more work and then lunch. Meals were very much as described by Fred Catherwood earlier—discussion could range around any topic, often one that caught his fancy, with the old lion stirring things up just to see what happened! Sometimes, though, he would simply share things that he had read.

For example, one meal time he talked about his interest in psychosomatic medicine—the case of the socialist who became paralysed in his left arm while doing military service, for instance—was it genuine paralysis, or something connected to his political convictions and a hidden unwillingness to recognise superior authority? (As Gaius Davies has shown in *The Doctor as a Doctor*, Dr Lloyd-Jones was interested in what we now call whole person medicine, and the relationship of the person to the individual complaint.)

He would sleep after lunch, not usually in bed, but in his favourite chair. Then there would be some more work on the sermons, and another game of croquet perhaps, or a game of snooker with Jonathan before some further manuscript work, followed by dinner. We would often then play a word game *en famille*, Lexicon being a particular favourite. Sometimes then there was television, simple quiet reading time, or a continuation of some earlier and very animated discussion. Finally, and often long after his poor son-in-law (who came from a family of larks) had grown weary and eager for bed, there would be family prayers, in which the Doctor himself naturally played a leading part, usually ending it by praying one of those extraordinary prayers which became so famous at Westminster Chapel. The whole counsel of God would appear in it, and the people prayed for would be from far and wide—and of course from the family as well. The larks would then retire to bed, while the owls stayed up, usually retiring finally around 12.30am to 1am.

Croquet was a major form of relaxation for him. When he died I lost not only a grandfather but also my croquet partner. It was physically relaxing of course, with a lot of walking in the fresh air. But it was also mentally helpful, as the mind was constantly alert. My grandmother Mrs Lloyd-Jones was a superb player, with over seventy years' experience when she herself died in 1991. I partnered my grandfather and my mother partnered my grandmother. Usually the ladies won, sometimes by a humiliating margin of 10–4, but more usually by 8–6. We played what is strictly described as 'golf croquet', a slightly more Christian version of the game, as each pair has a go for each hoop, unlike the official game in which a really good team can go through all fourteen hoops before the hapless other pair have even gone through the first. (If we had played that version, I think the Doctor and I would have been done for!) So the only way of ever beating the ladies was through tactics, and this the Doctor loved—it was the same when he played snooker with Jonathan. You could see him working things out in his mind as defeat loomed yet again! Of course we would win from time to time, and then the sense of triumph was considerable. Nemesis was around the corner, alas, as such things were often followed by a 10–4 defeat—the men could not get ideas above their station!

The whole family played Lexicon, though if my father was too busy with paperwork he had to opt out. The Lloyd-Joneses had played the game for years, having done so on a major train journey across North America in the 1930s. It was like a card version of Scrabble in some ways, except that the words did not have to join up. Each player had a go, but once that had happened— unless someone went out in one, which was very rare— one could add letters to already existing words held by other players. Here the two Scrabble experts—my mother and grandmother—usually reigned supreme, since they often played several Scrabble games a day and knew words of which none of us had ever heard! The Doctor and I usually did reasonably well, though seldom won, and the strength of the ladies was added to considerably as my sister grew more confident.

One thing the Doctor always did was to hand out the letter cards to each player at the beginning. Each of us had nine, and to make sure that there were no mistakes, he would call out the numbers as he did so—one, two, three, etc. When it came to number six, though, he would deliberately mispronounce it, making it sound—and the sound he made is virtually impossible to transcribe—like 'llillx', with the 'll' pronounced in the Welsh way, like the town of Llanelli. He always chortled at this point—both he and his brother Vincent had an endearing way of laughing at their own jokes, which made it just as well that they were usually funny!

In 1980 he was very ill. I spent much of that summer in the Far East, and while it would have been wonderful to be near him, in some ways I am glad that I was not there. One of his grandchildren, who took him for increasingly painful walks around the grounds, said that his arm was like a stick. It would not have been the kind of summer that we had known. So my memories of those wonderful summers in Balsham are only of him at his very best and most alert; of the Dacu I knew and loved, as did we all. Perhaps that is as it should be.

He died on my twenty-sixth birthday in 1981, having remembered the night before to tell my grandmother that he had thought about it. He thought of his grandchildren to the last and we have remembered him with the deepest affection ever since.

Notes

1. Christopher Catherwood, *Five Evangelical Leaders* (Wheaton: Harold Shaw, 1985), p. 58.
2. Iain Murray, *D. Martyn Lloyd-Jones: The First Forty Years, 1899–1939, vol. 1* (Edinburgh: The Banner of Truth Trust, 1982), p. 202.
3. *Ibid*, pp. 203–4.
4. *Ibid*, p. 205.
5. *Ibid*, p. 50.
6. Quotation from personal interview.
7. Charles Turner (ed.), *Chosen Vessels: Portraits of Ten Outstanding Christian Men* (Ann Arbor, Michigan: Servant Publications, 1985), p. 118.
8. *Ibid*, p. 119.
9. *Ibid*, p. 118.
10. Christopher Catherwood, *op. cit.*, p. 70.
11. *Ibid.*
12. *Ibid*, p. 71.
13. *Ibid.*
14. Charles Turner, *op. cit.*, p. 116.
15. *Ibid.*
16. Christopher Catherwood (ed.), *Chosen by God* (Crowborough: Highland Books, 1986), p. 210.
17. *Ibid*, p. 211.
18. *Ibid.*
19. *Ibid*, pp. 212–3.
20. *Ibid*, p. 215.
21. *Ibid*, p. 217.
22. *Ibid.*
23. *Ibid*, p. 225.
24. *Ibid*, pp. 225–6.
25. *Ibid*, p. 226.
26. *Ibid*, p. 37.
27. Christopher Catherwood, *Five Evangelical Leaders* (Wheaton: Harold Shaw, 1985), pp. 75–76.

28. Christopher Catherwood (ed.), *Chosen by God* (Crowborough: Highland Books, 1986), p. 112.
29. *Ibid*, p. 113.
30. Christopher Catherwood, *Five Evangelical Leaders* (Wheaton: Harold Shaw, 1985), p. 76.
31. *Ibid*.
32. *Ibid*, p. 77.
33. *Ibid*, p. 78.
34. Christopher Catherwood (ed.), *Chosen by God* (Crowborough: Highland Books, 1986), p. 115.
35. *Ibid*, pp. 115–116.
36. *Ibid*, p. 122.
37. *Ibid*, p. 123.
38. *Ibid*.
39. Christopher Catherwood, *Five Evangelical Leaders* (Wheaton: Harold Shaw, 1985), p. 76.
40. *Ibid*, p. 80.
41. *Ibid*.
42. Christopher Catherwood (ed.), *Chosen by God* (Crowborough: Highland Books, 1986), p. 117.
43. *Ibid*.
44. *Ibid*, pp. 117–118.
45. Martyn Lloyd-Jones, *Joy Unspeakable* (Eastbourne: Kingsway Publications, 1984), p. 16.
46. *Ibid*.
47. *Ibid*, p. 18.
48. *Ibid*.
49. *Ibid*, p. 19.
50. *Ibid*, p. 20.
51. *Ibid*, p. 21.
52. *Ibid*, p. 23.
53. *Ibid*, p. 28.
54. *Ibid*, p. 32.
55. *Ibid*, p. 201.
56. *Ibid*, p. 202.
57. *Ibid*, p. 203.
58. Christopher Catherwood, *Five Evangelical Leaders* (Wheaton: Harold Shaw, 1985), p. 129.
59. *Ibid*, p. 105.
60. Christopher Catherwood (ed.), *Chosen by God* (Crowborough: Highland Books, 1986), p. 220.
61. *Ibid*, p. 221.
62. *Ibid*.
63. *Ibid*.
64. *Ibid*, p. 222.
65. *Ibid*.
66. Martyn Lloyd-Jones, *op. cit.*, p. 19.

67. Christopher Catherwood (ed.), *Chosen by God* (Crowborough: Highland Books, 1986), p. 31.
68. Christopher Catherwood, *Five Evangelical Leaders* (Wheaton: Harold Shaw, 1985), pp. 78–79.
69. Christopher Catherwood (compiler), *The Best of Martyn Lloyd-Jones* (Eastbourne: Kingsway Publications, 1992), pp. 205, 207–208.
70. Iain Murray, *D. Martyn Lloyd-Jones: The Fight of Faith, 1939–1981*, vol. 11 (Edinburgh: The Banner of Truth Trust, 1990), p. 525.
71. Christopher Catherwood (ed.), *Chosen by God* (Crowborough: Highland Books, 1986), p. 207.
72. Iain Murray, *D. Martyn Lloyd-Jones: The Fight of Faith, 1939–1981*, vol. 11 (Edinburgh: The Banner of Truth Trust, 1990), p. 525.
73. *Ibid*, p. 527.
74. Charles Turner (ed.), *Chosen Vessels: Portraits of Ten Outstanding Christian Men* (Ann Arbor, Michigan: Servant Publications, 1985), pp. 109–110.
75. *Ibid*, p. 112.
76. Christopher Catherwood (ed.), *Chosen by God* (Crowborough: Highland Books, 1986), pp. 49–50.
77. Christopher Catherwood, *Five Evangelical Leaders* (Wheaton: Harold Shaw, 1985), p. 88.
78. *Ibid*, pp. 88–89.
79. Charles Turner, *op. cit.*, p. 112.
80. Iain Murray, *D. Martyn Lloyd-Jones: The Fight of Faith, 1939–1981*, vol. 11 (Edinburgh: The Banner of Truth Trust, 1990), p. 538.
81. *Ibid*, p. 540.
82. Christopher Catherwood (ed.), *Chosen by God* (Crowborough: Highland Books, 1986), pp. 24–25.
83. *Ibid*, p. 27.
84. *Ibid*, pp. 27–28.
85. Charles Turner, *op. cit.*, p. 123.
86. *Ibid*.
87. *Ibid*, p. 121.
88. *Ibid*, p. 122.
89. *Ibid*.
90. Christopher Catherwood (ed.), *Chosen by God* (Crowborough: Highland Books, 1986), pp. 63–64.
91. *Ibid*, p. 206.
92. *Ibid*, p. 131.

Bibliography

Catherwood, Christopher, *Five Evangelical Leaders* (Wheaton: Harold Shaw, 1985. New edition: Christian Focus Publications, 1994).

Catherwood, Christopher (compiler), *The Best of Martyn Lloyd-Jones* (Eastbourne: Kingsway Publications, 1992).

Catherwood, Christopher (ed.), *Chosen by God* (Crowborough: Highland Books, 1986).

Lloyd-Jones, Martyn, *Joy Unspeakable* (Eastbourne: Kingsway Publications, 1984).

Murray, Iain, *D. Martyn Lloyd-Jones: The First Forty Years, 1899–1939 vol. 1* (Edinburgh: The Banner of Truth Trust, 1982).

Murray, Iain, *D. Martyn Lloyd-Jones: The Fight of Faith, 1939–1981, vol. 2* (Edinburgh: The Banner of Truth Trust, 1990).

Turner, Charles (ed.), *Chosen Vessels: Portraits of Ten Outstanding Christian Men* (Ann Arbor, Michigan: Servant Publications, 1985).

Index